CW00621365

POCKET IMAGES

Doncaster's Town & Country Houses

Campsall Hall in ruins, 1980. (Photograph by Eric Braim)

POCKET IMAGES

Doncaster's Town & Country Houses

Peter Tuffrey

NONSUCH

The author
pictured
in Hooton
Pagnell Hall,
around 1976.

For W.H. Gordon Smith—thanks for your help and support over the years.

First published 2000
This new pocket edition 2007
Images unchanged from first edition

Nonsuch Publishing Limited
Cirencester Road, Chalford,
Stroud, Gloucestershire, GL6 8PE
www.nonsuch-publishing.com

Nonsuch Publishing is an imprint of NPI Media Group

British Library Cataloguing in Publication Data.
A catalogue record for this book is available from the British Library.

ISBN 978-1-84588-398-0

Typesetting and origination by Nonsuch Publishing Limited
Printed in Great Britain by Oaklands Book Services Limited

Contents

Acknowledgements

I would also like to thank Eric Braim for help with the text and supplying a number of photographs. Gratitude must also be expressed to Malcom Barnsdale, Jim Collins, Philip Langford, Trevor Miller, the late Gerry Seymour, and Jim Wilson.

Aerial view of Beechfield House, Waterdale, c.1930.

Introduction

It was during 1975 that I first became aware of the large number of town and country houses which had existed, or were still in existence, in and around Doncaster. It was my first year as Keeper of Art at Doncaster Museum & Art Gallery and I was organizing an exhibition of local historian, W.H. Gordon Smith's impressive photographs of Doncaster's houses, mansions and country estates.

Besides working for the Civil Service, Gordon was agent to the Old Cusworth Estate and, during the 1960s he wrote a splendid series on Doncaster's country houses for the now defunct *Doncaster Gazette*. Gordon has also produced several books: *Sprotbrough Hall, Askern Spa, Cusworth Hall and the Battie-Wrightson Family, Sprotbrough Colliery, Campsall Hall* (unpublished) and *Cantley Hall* (unpublished). The exhibition featured some photographs taken by G.W. Taylor during the mid-nineteenth century, and these are probably some of the earliest examples of the photographers' art in Doncaster. The most interesting of these was a picture of the old Brodsworth Hall, taken before the new structure was erected.

A little later, I was part of a team which organized an exhibition at Doncaster called 'The Destruction of the English Country House.' The core items in the show came from a Victoria & Albert Museum touring exhibition of the same title. Doncaster augmented the exhibition with a number of impressive objects from the small number of houses still remaining in the area including Brodsworth Hall, Hooton Pagnell Hall, Sandbeck Park and Womersley Hall. My job was to supervise the transportation, documentation and display of the objects from these houses. In doing so, it gave me the unique opportunity to visit these vast private houses, and their titled occupants. At Womersley, the regal Lady De Vesci, who was in her nineties told me to be relaxed and not to worry about the possibility of dropping one of the priceless Sèvres vases: 'If you drop one, you drop it, and that will be the end of that, don't worry,' she quipped. Needless to say, I didn't drop anything, handling and packing the objects with extreme care. Betty Warde-Norbury at Hooton Pagnell was great fun. I had lunch with her quite a few times and many interesting chats. In fact she took the picture of me at the Hall, which is reproduced on page 4. I found Silvia Grant Dalton at Brodsworth Hall quite an eccentric lady, but took tea with her on several occasions, and saw every nook and cranny of Brodsworth before it was restored by English Heritage. A mention should also be made of her chef, George, who I understood once worked for Mountbatten and the Spencers. 'I knew Lady Diana when she was a child,' he boasted to me in later years. Lord Scarborough at Sandbeck was very friendly indeed, proudly allowing me to see many items from his family heritage.

Since that time, in the mid-1970s, I have gathered my own collection of pictures of Doncaster's town and country houses, and related pieces of information from newspapers and books. I have collaborated with Gordon Smith on several projects, and in 1988, he took me to visit the ageing Mrs Maureen Pearse (formerly Barbara Isabella Georgiana Battie-Wrightson) in London. She was ninety-eight at the time, and the last of the line of the Battie-Wrightsons. Her mother, Lady Isabella, is featured on the front cover of this book.

In 1996, I wrote a series for the *Doncaster Star* titled 'Peter Tuffrey Tours Doncaster's Town and Country Houses', an article appearing each week for just over a year. In producing this I was indebted to both Gordon Smith and Eric Braim, Secretary of Doncaster Civic Trust, who has produced many splendid articles on Doncaster's architectural history. This book is an edited version of the *Star* series and I am grateful to Nonsuch Publishing for producing it in this form. There are one or two houses featured in here which did not appear in the newspaper series including Bessacarr Grange, Edenfield and Wilsic Hall, so this provides the book with an added bonus. The photographs are from the lenses of a number of photographers: G.W. Taylor, Edgar Leonard Scrivens and Eric Braim.

Hopefully, when readers peruse this book they will find it a useful and informative record of Doncaster's once rich heritage of town and country houses.

Peter Tuffrey
June 2000

Adwick-le-Street Rectory was purchased in 1952 by Adwick-le-Street UDC to house the treasurer's department. The transfer took place in August 1954, the rest of the UDC departments remaining in the old council offices in Village Street. During the following year, the new Council Chamber was completed and an official opening took place on 6 December 1955.

A booklet, published to coincide with the building's opening as a town hall, included the following: '[The building] dates back to the reign of King Charles the Second, to be precise the year 1682. One Albrede de Lisureo gave the 'glebe' of St Laurence Church to the Nunnery at Hampole, but after the dissolution of that Order, a Mrs Anne Saville of Methley purchased it at a cost of £900 and settled it on the church forever. The Revd Joshua Brooke being the incumbent and having his income considerably enlarged by the addition of [that] benefice, built at his own cost [in 1682] the present parsonage house from the foundation.'

Above: Alverley Hall, now demolished, but formerly situated near Edlington Wood, was built towards the end of the eighteenth century by a Joseph Dixon, previously resident at Wadworth. After his death, the property was bought by Thomas Bradford, a member of Doncaster Corporation, who in turn sold the estate to Brian Darwin Cooke, a member of the same family as the owners of the Wheatley Hall estate. He enlarged and generally improved the house, and it remained with the Cooke family until after the death of F.G. Cooke. His heir, the Revd Charles Cooke then sold the Alverley estate to Reginald Thompson, a member of the Bradford brewing firm, and from him it passed into the hands of the West Riding County Council. At the time that the council took possession of the property, there was on the estate, in addition to the Hall, one farmstead, which had been occupied by the Nicholson brothers, the Doncaster maltsters and their father before them, for over half a century. The Hall was then leased to a Mr Smith of the Balby Wire Works. The Alverley estate was offered for sale during June 1889, and subsequent tenants at the Hall have included Major Elgerton and a Mr Ellis. The Hall experienced mixed fortunes during the twentieth century; the estate being used at one time for smallholdings.

Opposite: Shortly after the First World War, there was a proposal to use the Hall as a convalescent home. However, when all the arrangements were well advanced, the Pensions Ministry announced that they had decided not to proceed with the scheme. Later, the Hall was used 'as a Summer School for training young women for rural areas.' On 28 January 1927 the *Doncaster Gazette* announced that Alverley Hall, once run as a farming college, 'is now occupied by a number of families working at the nearby village of Edlington.' Colin Walton in the *Doncaster Free Press*, 13 December 1984, recounts the final years of the Hall: 'During the Second World War the area, including the House, was used by the ARP as a training ground. Vandalism completed the work of time, subsidence and the elements. The roof and floors of the building had disappeared ... These pathetic remains overlooked an equally derelict cluster of outbuildings. Now Alverley House has disappeared completely and with it the memories of a forgotten age rich in elegance and style.' The two pictures reproduced here include female agricultural students posing outside the Hall.

Arksey Hall, a two-storey cement rendered property has reputedly 'a Tudor core,' according to Magilton (1977). He also adds that the Hall has an internal feature dated 1653, but the remainder is probably Georgian, though the roof is modern. The porch features two Doric Columns, while an adjacent two-storeyed outbuilding is probably contemporary with the final alteration to the Hall around 1820. In the *Doncaster Gazette*, 26 January 1967, Gordon Smith notes: 'For a time the [Arksey Estate] was held by Godfrey Copley of Sprotbrough Hall (who died in 1634) and passed Arksey to his cousin Mary, the wife of Edmund Hastings. The Hastings family resided there until 1654, when it was purchased by Bryan Cooke of Wheatley Hall and for over the next 200 years continued to form part of the Wheatley Estate.' One of Arksey Hall's noted squires was William Chadwick JP. His long, informative obituary in the *Doncaster Chronicle*, 1 April 1910, included the following: 'He was known more through his connection with various public institutions, governing bodies, and organisations, and for the liberality with which he subscribed to and supported certain objects, than for the style he maintained at Arksey Hall, the way in which he entertained, or the manner in which he passed his long hours of leisure ... The late Mr Chadwick was the eldest and only surviving son of the late William Chadwick, from whom he inherited Arksey Hall and estates.' Chadwick was born at Arksey and lived there as a bachelor for most of his life though he did frequently tour abroad and the Hall reputedly contained evidence of that. Gordon Smith mentions that at the time of writing, Arksey was privately owned, though divided in two; the rear portion being used by Denbigh's Cleaners as their area headquarters. Since that time, the Hall has become a nursing home.

Most people associate Austerfield Manor House with the Bradford family, but Malcolm Dolby in his *William Bradford of Austerfield* (Mayflower Pilgrim 1589/90–1657) states: 'Although the Manor House contains elements of timber framing, and would have existed as a totally timber-framed structure in Bradford's time, there is unfortunately no substantiation for the tradition which can be traced back no further than the mid-19th century.' However, an article in the *Doncaster Chronicle*, 22 June 1950, mentions, 'It is true that Bradford once owned the Old Manor because his name appears in the title deeds. Tradition also says that the Pilgrim Fathers, then called the separatists, held their meetings in the Old Manor cellar. There is now no evidence of a secret entry, though the arched roof and compact squareness of the room breathe of this anxious past.' The 1950 article also notes that the old manor house was condemned as uninhabitable in 1937, but was being restored by Lt-Col. W. Forrest Bracewell.

The photograph shows Ashmount, High Road Balby, before conversion to a Working Men's Club. The club founded in 1908, was affiliated in 1912. Since being occupied by the club, stone cladding has been added to the building's frontage.

St Catherine's Hall, Balby, was erected around 1827 by wool merchant George Banks of Hunslet, Leeds. An anonymous manuscript entitled 'The St Catherine's Estate', tells us that although George Banks remained a bachelor, he had a daughter by Elizabeth King in 1829. The child was given the name Georgiana, and he made her his sole beneficiary. George came to Loversall with

his daughter Georgiana and sister Elizabeth Goodman, dying there in 1845. Georgiana married the vicar of Loversall when she was eighteen and he twenty-six, becoming Mrs Robert Sharpe. However by 1854 the vicar had taken the name of Banks. They left the Hall with their seven children in 1866, leasing it to a variety of tenants, including a family called Williams, a Mr Charles Stephen Cooke, and a Mr and Mrs Mathews. 'After they left, the Banks' returned to St Catherine's. The vicar's second child, George James Banks (born 1850), a barrister, moved there.'

Above and below: The St Catherine's estate was put up for sale in 1887, but was not sold. After George James's death in 1901, members of the Banks family continued to live at the Hall until it was purchased by a consortium of Doncaster businessmen, intending to develop the area, of some 100 acres, for building purposes. There was a sale of antique furniture, china paintings and books from the Hall in 1928. The well-known art buyer, Mr Sabin, was amongst those purchasing items.

In 1932, the Hall was acquired by the local Health Authority, becoming a home for 'mental defectives'. It has remained with the Health department since that time, though sadly one of the lodges was demolished during the 1970s.

Westfield House, in Fisher's Park, Balby. This house was built during the early nineteenth century and was for many years the residence of Frederick Fisher, Doncaster's town clerk from 1824 to 1835, and afterwards his son, F.W. Fisher, clerk to the Borough magistrates. The widow of the latter survived him for many years, but after her death, negotiations for the purchase of the estate were concluded in 1937 by the Doncaster Corporation. Shortly afterwards, the House was demolished, the grounds being utilized as a park. In 1913, two people were charged with an attempted 'suffragist outrage' at Westfield House.

Barnburgh Grange, was situated off the road to High Melton, and while the building depicted here was of considerable age, it was not according to J.S. Large in the *History of Barnburgh* (1952), the original building. He also adds, 'From time to time the Religious Houses acquired land by bequests and endowments and as these grew in size it often became necessary for them to set up a grange and employ a granger (or bailiff) to look after the land. Barnburgh Grange was

part of Nostell Priory in whose possession it had been for over three centuries at the time of the dissolution.' When Barnburgh Grange was demolished in July 1965, it was owned by Mexborough UDC, having been acquired in 1928 to be used as a farmhouse.

'[Barnburgh Hall] is in a retired situation, and a short distance from the church ... The building, which was greatly modernised by Basil More, Esq., still retains much of its original character. It is of considerable extent, and delightfully situated; looking eastwards over undulating ground, cultivated fields and luxuriant woodland foliage. The front presents three characteristic gables, the windows of which exhibit traces of comparatively recent alteration, with a low and wide doorway in the centre, still possessing, there is every reason to believe, its former appearance.' This is how C.W. Hatfield described Barnburgh Hall, now demolished, in his *Village Sketches Hints to Pedestrians* reprinted from the *Doncaster Gazette*, 1849-1850.

L.S.85-6 The Hall, Barnborough, From The Gardens.

Perhaps Barnburgh Hall is most noted for its connection with Sir Thomas More, the Lord Chancellor of Henry VIII's reign. Sir Thomas, according to the *Doncaster Chronicle*, 27 May 1932: 'came to Barnburgh to affect a marriage between his only son John, and Anne Cresacre, the only daughter and heiress to the estates of the Knightly family of that name who occupied the Hall for generations.' After the marriage, the newspaper alleged that Sir Thomas was a fairly frequent visitor to the Hall. For generations a picture has hung in the house, 'showing Sir Thomas, his son and his wife, and tradition held that the painting was by Hans Holbein.' In fact Hatfield goes some way to confirm this. 'Hans Holbein, most likely accompanied Sir Thomas thither [to Barnburgh Hall].'

Not many writers have made pertinent comments about the Hall's architectural antiquity, the exception possibly being Winifred Hayward in *The Secret Rooms of Yorkshire* (1956). She wrote, 'Early in the Tudor period [the Cresacre family] transformed their manor-house into a more comfortable mansion, ranged round three sides of a small courtyard ... In the eighteenth century the house was very much altered, but when the interior was reconstructed, the Tudor Stone walls were not destroyed but merely screened with plaster and panelling, and fireplaces inserted in front of the Tudor ones.' Naturally the Hall was not without its nooks and crannies, not to mention secret rooms and a ghost! The Revd W.J. Parker in *The Cresacre Treasure: The Church and Village of Barnburgh* (undated) gives the following details: 'The Hall was often used in troubled times of the sixteenth century as a refuge by Roman Catholics and priests. It contained a secret room on the first floor, with a window slit only the width of the plaster on the outside but widening inwards. In the secret room was a loose floor below which was a priest's hole, entered by a rope ladder. This was at the side of the Dining Room fireplace and a sliding panel in the wall was used for passing food to the fugitive. The Hall is said to be haunted by a ghost that frequents the organ loft half way up the staircase.'

Descendants of the More family continued in possession of the Barnburgh property until the early nineteenth century, the last to reside at the Hall being Thomas Peter More. Henrietta Griffith lived there in 1815, remaining until 1835 when the property was leased to the Hartop family. It was sold to the Montagus in 1859, though the Hartops continued to live there until 1911. The Hall's tenants after them included Bernard H. Thompson, a son of the late Archbishop of York, and the Doncaster Collieries Association. One of the latter's chief officials who resided at the Hall was Capt. C.L.C. Hodges. During its later years the Hall's occupants were Mr and Mrs G.C. Payne. The Hall was demolished amidst much controversy during the late 1960s.

C.W. Hatfield noted: 'The [Barnburgh] Rectory House, which has been recently taken down, stood on the south-eastern side of the [church], and on its pleasant site another is now (1849) in the course of erection by Messrs Anelay of Doncaster, builders.' The new building, pictured here, having an extensive view overlooking surrounding villages, was constructed during the time of the Revd Thomas Cozens Percival, rector between 1848 and 1863.

Above and below: The Grove at Barnby Dun once stood adjacent to the church, amidst a large garden and some fine trees. It has been speculated upon that it was built as a hunting box (lodge). The occupants during the ninenteeth century included Thomas Gresham, Baron Rendlesham, James Newsome, and J.H. Newsome. From a sale notice in 1874, we can glean that the property included ten bedrooms, a pinery, vinery, conservatory, shrubbery and rookery. In 1940, the house was bought by the Doncaster Amalgamated Collieries, passing to the National Coal Board in 1946.

Controversy raged in the mid-1980s when the house was demolished. The *Doncaster Civic Trust Newsletter*, No. 48 of March 1986 stated: 'Some villagers, hearing that a builder had bought the House with an eye to redevelopment, turned to the Trust for help in saving the House. The Trust agreed to try and get the house 'listed' but the Department of the Enviroment refused to do so, presumably because of the alterations that had been made to the House ...

the aforementioned builder who, having obtained planning permission for the erection of several houses on the site, has recently razed Grove House to the ground.'

According to Joseph Hunter in his *South Yorkshire: The Deanery of Doncaster* (2 vols, 1828, 1831), the greater part of the present Bawtry Hall was built following the sale in 1779 of Bawtry Manor to prominent west Yorkshire politician Pemberton Milnes. This suggests that parts of an existing house were incorporated into the new one. Hunter probably assumed this from reading Bawtry historian, William Peck's *A Topographical History of Bawtry and Thorne with Villages Adjacent* (1813), since it states: 'The old part of a family mansion was taken down [presumably by Pemberton Milnes] and the present structure erected on its site.' Following Milnes' death in 1795, his daughter Bridget inherited the Bawtry estate. She resided at the Hall with her first husband Peter Auriol Hay Drummond until his untimely death at the age of forty-five in 1799. In 1803, Bridget married Robert Monkton Arundel, 4th Viscount Galway, of Serlby Hall, which is where the couple principally resided. Bawtry was maintained as a second house, but after his death in 1810, Bridget appears to have stayed principally at Bawtry.

When Bridget died in 1835, the Hall's principal residents during the remainder of the century included Robert Pemberton Milnes, nephew of Pemberton Milnes and MP for Pontefract; a railway director; a Roman Catholic family named Gandolfi who set aside a room for an oratory; Richard Monkton Milnes MP for Pontefract; Charles Hugh Lowther; MP James Lowther; William Gerard Lysley; and L. Threlfall Baines.

The Hall's most notable occupant during the twentieth century, and indeed the last private owner of Bawtry Hall, was Maj. George H. Peake, who purchased the property in 1904 from the Earl of Crewe, who it is believed never resided at Bawtry. Peake was born in 1859 and married Evelyn Mary Dundas in 1895. He added a wing to the Hall at the rear around 1905, incorporating a water tower. His wife who features in the above picture was quite a noted local personality.

Maj. and Mrs Peake vacated the Hall at the outbreak of the Second World War, making Sutton Hall, Thirsk, their home. Mrs Peake died in 1945, her husband five years later. Bawtry Hall was occupied from 1939 by the West Kent Regiment until 1941, when it was taken over by the RAF and used by them as the headquarters of No. 1 (Bomber) Group. Further additions were made to the Hall by the RAF, both as an Operations Centre and Meteorological Office. During the 1980s, the Hall was vacated by the RAF and subsequently occupied by the Christians Reaching the World organization.

On 10 February 1981 the *Doncaster Evening Post* reported that conservation volunteers were offering to preserve Bessacarr Grange, Doncaster Council's unique Victorian farm, which the council at one time threatened to demolish. All they wanted the Council to do was to grant them a short term licence so they could show they were capable of looking after the property, and then a longer term lease so that they could embark on a proper restoration scheme. Magilton (1977) stated: 'House is derelict with Welsh slate roof. Sash windows in late-eighteenth-century style. Entrance to courtyard has dovecote in pediment.'

Eric Braim in the *Doncaster Civic Trust Newsletter*, No. 45 of March 1985 mentions that the designs for Bilham Belvedere, near Hickleton were exhibited at the Royal Academy in 1800 by John Rawstorne. In the *Newsletter* of October 1994, Eric Braim mentioned that Bilham Belvedere on the Brodsworth Estate was one of twenty miscellaneous buildings at risk. 'The cost of repairs deterred the Landmark Trust in 1990 but it would still make an idyllic dwelling.'

Opposite above: Eric Braim in the *Doncaster Civic Trust Newsletter*, 26 November 1978, informs that Bessacarr Grange was built with an eye for symmetry and classical proportions by B.W.D. Cooke around 1800. Cooke had previously consulted Humphrey Repton, the famous landscape architect, about the laying out of his estate at Bessacarr.

Opposite below: *The Doncaster Star*, 27 January 1988, mentioned that planning bosses were holding up the final demolition of an historic farmhouse in Doncaster. 'Bessacarr Grange farmhouse was found partially-collapsed last summer after its outbuildings and barns were demolished. These were levelled with the consent of a planning inspector, but he ruled the farmhouse must remain for conversion and restoration. How it came to collapse was still being investigated.' In subsequent years the area was cleared.

Blyth Hall was once described as a 'beautiful William and Mary mansion,' being built by Edward Mellish in 1684–1685. Architectural details are aptly supplied by Nikolaus Pevsner in his *Buildings of England Nottinghamshire* (1951): '[Blyth Hall] was seven bays wide with north and south façades both with a centre of five bays and one-bay projections at each end and then one outer bay. H.M. Calvin suggests an attribution on stylistic grounds to Talman. Carr added a bay-window drawing room with Adamish detail between two towers in the 1770s (payments 1773 and 1776) ... Quoins and (perhaps also around 1770) square turrets in the Burlingtonian taste on the four projections.'

The Revd John Raine in his *The History and Antiquities of the Parish of Blyth* (1860) gives details of the building of the Hall and the materials used. 'In 1684, [Edward Mellish] began to take down the old residence of Blyth Abbey, and in April of that year commenced building the present Blyth Hall ... The timber was brought from Sandbeck Park, and consisted of forty-two trees ... The bricks were made upon Lindrick Common.'

Perhaps the best-known descendent of Edward Mellish's to occupy Blyth Hall was Henry 'Madcap' Mellish. He came into possession of the extensive Blyth estates at the age of twenty-one in 1803. According to the *Doncaster Gazette*, 25 August 1960, he was 'a true Regency Rake, but it was said an honourable one.'

Right: The Madcap died of dropsy on 24 July 1817 aged thirty-seven and was buried at Blyth. The House was subsequently sold to Joshua Walker of Clifton, Rotherham, son of the founder of the Masborough ironworks. It remained with his family until 1888.

Below: Blyth Hall was eventually purchased by Lord Barnby of Barnby Moor, head of the firm of Francis Willey & Co. wool merchants of Bradford, London and Boston USA. Like Henry Mellish before him, Lord Barnby was a horse lover, establishing a stud at Blyth. Also, similar to Mellish, Lord Barnby entertained well at the Hall. After Lord Barnby's death, Blyth Hall was bought, along with the rest of the estate, by E. Bartlett of Exeter, though he subsequently put it up for auction. Even though the estate was sold, the Hall was under a serious threat of demolition for a time. However, the *Doncaster Gazette*, 25 July 1930 stated: 'Blyth Hall has been saved, the roofed shell having been bought for £675 by J.C. Lister of Listerdale Rotherham.' However, the Hall subsequently fell into ruins and finally succumbed to the demolition hammer in 1972.

The Manor, Braithwell a two-storey property with mullion windows, said to date from the late seventeeth century, but having the appearance of a nineteenth-century vicarage.

The Rectory, Braithwell, a nineteenth-century structure.

On 29 March 1861 the *Doncaster Gazette* reported: 'C.C. Thellusson Esq., the present owner of the Brodsworth estate, is about to erect a new hall, on a site a short distance from the present mansion, and which will command a fine view of the adjoining countryside. The contract was let a few days ago, at the sum, it is stated, of somewhere about £20,000.' The new Hall was designed by Chevalier Casentini, but according to Caroline Whitworth in the 'Brodsworth Hall' catalogue: 'the actual building was undertaken by [contractors Longmire & Barge] at the direction of a London architect, Philip Wilkinson.'

On 9 August 1861, the *Doncaster Gazette* wrote about an accident at Brodsworth. William Lindley of Factory Lane, Doncaster, and foreman of the labourers employed in the extensive alterations being made at Brodsworth Hall, had had a serious accident. 'He was pulling down the ceiling of one of the rooms [presumably of the old Hall], when it gave way, and, knocking him off the scaffold, fell upon his chest and injured him severely.' Both pictures on this page show the old Brodsworth Hall.

On Friday 25 April 1862, another incident made news in the *Doncaster Gazette*, after a fatal accident had occurred at Brodsworth on the Wednesday, to thirty-seven year old, John Hall, the foreman of the stone masons for Messrs Longmire & Barge, contractors employed in the re-erection of the Hall. The deceased had superintended the stone work generally and under his direction the portico had been erected. It was built of stone from the Brodsworth quarries, and the supports of the portico, inserted in the wall, and extending there from more than twelve inches, were of the same quality. On the Tuesday night he directed their removal, as in his opinion the cement was sufficiently set.

On 2 May 1862, the *Doncaster Gazette*, seemingly oblivious to the construction of the Hall's cost in human terms, reported: 'The damage sustained by the fall of the portico at Brodsworth Hall, the seat of Charles S.A. Thellusson, Esq., will be little short of £800. Mr Taylor, of St Sepulchre-gate, has, we perceive, taken a photograph of the east view of the House after the accident.' The picture above shows the Hall gardens.

The Hall was completed by 1863–1864, and was occupied by the Thellusons until 1931, when it passed to the Grant Daltons. Members of this family stayed at the Hall for nearly sixty years, which was then given to English Heritage in 1990. Over the following five years, the Hall underwent an extensive restoration and conservation programme, before opening to the public in 1995. The above pictures depict Charles Thellusson and his wife Constance.

A view of the Bothy, used by the gardeners, in the Hall gardens.

Left: Charles Grant-Dalton (born 1884) succeeded to the Brodsworth estate in 1931 following the death of Augustus Thellusson. Earlier, in 1916, Charles had married Silvia West (born 1901), and they had one daughter, Pamela. Charles died in 1952, and Silvia subsequently married, in 1959, his cousin Eustace Foster Grant-Dalton (born 1877), who survived until 1970. Thereafter Silvia, who is pictured here, continued to live at Brodsworth until her own death in 1988.

Below: A view of the Hall gardens.

According to Miller (1804): 'Burghwallis Hall has roof timbers of Tudor origin, though the south west wing was built by George Anne about 1797.' It was a typical eighteenth-century house with five bays and a centre three-bay roof pediment. The exterior was stuccoed, which remained until about 1820 when Michael Anne altered the exterior to give it a medieval look, removing all the stucco and revealing the stone beneath it. Around the same time, Michael Tasburgh-Anne built the front staircase and the south-west chapel wing, destroying the original 'attic' chapel. A priest, who regularly appeared from Doncaster and Pontefract during the eighteenth and nineteenth centuries, carried out services in the new chapel. This was closed from 1888, as the Hall was being let to Protestants.

In 1907 the Anne family returned to Burgwallis. A year later Crawthorne Anne discovered a priest's hiding hole, secretly accessible from the chapel. George Anne left the Hall to his nephew Ernest Charlton, on the understanding that he took the Anne surname. Ernest's son, Maj. George Anne, was the Hall's last resident, selling it for a mere £1,000 in 1941.

The House was later acquired by the Sisters of Charity of Our Lady of Good and Perpetual Succour, taking care of old and infirm ladies. The mansion was then known as St Anne's Convent. The Hall gates are seen in the above picture.

233.3. The Rectory. Burghwallis.

Magilton (1977) noted that Burghwallis Rectory dated largely from the eighteenth century, containing a slate roof, sash windows, cement rendered walls, and that it was pedimented on the side elevations. He also mentioned that the nineteenth-century three-storey east wing was 'huge and ugly.'

For a long time, Campsall Hall was the home of the Bacon Frank family, and had a chequered history before being demolished in 1984. The Frank side of the family were settled at Grimsby in the reign of Edward II. By marriage and purchase they acquired properties in Yorkshire at Balne, Askern, Pontefract and Fenwick, and in 1625 Richard Frank bought Campsall, making it the family home. The addition of Bacon to the surname is a little complicated, but was explained by the *Doncaster Chronicle*, 4 January 1951: 'The three sons of Richard Frank died young and the estates passed to Edward Aston, the son of his elder daughter. Edward Aston's brother, Mathew, succeeded him and when Mathew's second son Francis married Elizabeth, daughter and heiress of Waller Bacon, of Earlham, Norfolk, the name Bacon Frank originated. Their son, Bacon, born in 1739, eventually succeeded to Campsall around 1762. A year later he married and began altering the Hall which, hitherto, had been a long narrow building.'

The picture to the right shows, from left to right, back row: the second Mrs Frederick Bacon Frank, the first Mrs Frederick Bacon Frank, Frederick Bacon Frank. Front row: Baldwin Peel, Baldwin Peel's half-sister.

Edward Frank was succeeded on his death in 1834 by his grandson Frederick Bacon Frank, then only five years old. Shortly before Frederick's inheritance, and for a period afterwards, the Hall was tenanted by a number of individuals including the naturalist Charles Thorold Wood. Frederick was responsible for alterations at Campsall Hall during the 1860s. He died in 1911, leaving the Hall and estates to his second wife, some thirty-two years his junior. There were no children by either of his marriages.

In 1942, Frederick's second wife died and according to her obituary in the *Doncaster Chronicle*, 5 March 1942: 'Mrs Bacon had not lived at Campsall since before the War, but despite her age, had visited her old home every summer to see her many friends.' Her heir was Miss Helen Marjorie Walker, her late husband's cousin and her one time companion. Miss Walker took over Campsall but lived at the retreat in York until her death in 1971.'

Right: On 13 August 1942 the *Doncaster Chronicle* reported on a sale of manuscripts from Campsall Hall at Sotherby's that raised £3,337. 'An immense interest centred on Henry V's manuscript of Chaucer's *Troilus and Criseyde* of which only two examples still remain in private hands ... There were letters of Queen Elizabeth, James I, the Earl of Leicester, Sir Walter Raleigh and other documents of historic interest ...' The picture here shows a doorway at Campsall Hall.

Below: The *Doncaster Chronicle* ran an article on 4 January 1951 about Campsall Hall entitled '*Fate of Another Hall in the Balance*' and on 31 May of the same year, reported on a proposal to turn the House into flats and a home for aged people. 'Doncaster RDC on Saturday agreed to issue licenses to the Campsall and Earlham Estates Co. for work to begin on the drainage system at a cost of £500. They further recommended that the Ministry of Works be asked to issue licences in respect of an application by the company for the conversion of the Hall at a cost of £2,750.'

In 1957 the Hall's lodges and gates were under threat, noted in the *Doncaster Chronicle* of 21 March. 'Doncaster RDC on Saturday deferred consideration of the future of the lodges and gates at Campsall Park ... The County Council offered no objection to the demolition of the lodges but considered that the iron gates and supporting pillars had sufficient architectural merit to warrant their preservation.' The picture here shows the Hall around 1983.

During the 1970s the future of Campsall Hall began to look uncertain. In 1979, Eric Braim noted in the *Doncaster Civic Trust News Letter* No 29: 'The Trust expressed its concern, some time since, to the Department of the Enviroment about the continuing deterioration of the fabric of the building and at the lack of effort to keep out vandals who were causing tremendous damage to the Hall.' In 1984, Campsall Hall, the stables and coach house were razed to the ground.

.L.S. 45-9. THE VICARAGE, CAMPSALL.

According to Magilton (1977): '[Campsall Rectory/Vicarage] is [a] T-shaped 15 century Manor House, altered about 1800. [It] may have been connected with Norton 'Priory'. Chapel window is preserved, signs of N. window and doorway into chapel ...' The *Doncaster Gazette*, 27 April adds more detail: 'The present Vicarage was, in fact, a church house belonging to the Priory of Burghwallis, and dating back to 1300. Outside in the yard you can see a good example of a perpendicular window, now bricked up, which once lit up the room now reputed to be haunted.' This story dates from 1905 when a female district visitor was forced to stay the night at the vicarage. In the early morning her screams alarmed the household, and before the vicar and his wife could rise she was beating at the door of their room. She had awakened to find a man in the room in an old fashioned costume, with a large wig and hands, dressed somewhat like a picture of Dr Johnson she had seen. He had a sword in his hand, and was in a watchful attitude at the window. She said he looked like a madman and when he gripped her, he felt deathly cold. She had managed to scream and rush from the room. It was discovered later on that in the time of Queen Anne, the vicar at that time was deprived of his living for some misdemeanour, but refused to give up the possession of the vicarage. The newly appointed vicar therefore tried to effect entry into the vicarage by means of a ladder leading to the window, but he was murdered while doing so by the old vicar, who was standing guard by the window with a sword. The old vicar was later hanged and it was presumed that the uncanny visitor was the wicked and murderous vicar. Neither the district visitor, nor the vicar in 1905, knew anything about the tragedy in Queen Anne's time.

Campsmount, now demolished, was situated on a hill, west of Campsall village. The house was built between 1752 and 1756 by Robert Carr for Thomas Yarbrough. The house was very plain in appearance but this was used to good effect. Yarbrough had said the following in 1753 about the design he had decided upon: 'A plain regular building composed with all the beauty of order is beyond all carving and ornaments.' Before the new house was conceived, the Yarbrough family occupied Brayton Hall, a short distance north-west of Campsmount, u-shaped and built around 1580. An article by Timothy Connor 'The Building of Campsmount' published in the *Yorkshire Archaeological Journal* Vol. 47 1975, charts the progress of the new house's construction. 'Before embarking on the new house project, Thomas Yarbrough spent much time erecting and improving farm buildings and properties occupied by his tenants. He then employed Joseph Perfect to make improvements to the landscape into which Campsmount was subsequently blended. A summer house was also built.' Timothy Connor argues that account books suggest Yarborough probably thought about building a new house because Brayton Hall was requiring more and more attention. In 1728, Yarborough paid £110 10s to John Howgill, a York carver, to draw a plan of a new house, yet nothing more can be gleaned about the idea until 1750–1751 when he paid John Carr for producing plans and elevations of a proposed house to be built at Campsall. John's father Robert Carr delivered an estimate for a new house which amounted to £4,707. Yarborough also paid a 'Mr Pain for sketching a plan for a house.'

Above and below: Eventually, Yarborough trusted Robert and his father to organize the new house's construction. He moved into his new property around February 1756 and wrote: 'The unity and regularity of the design which reigns everywhere about it. A new erection, a new name—Campsmount.' Yarborough died in 1772 at the age of eighty-five, leaving two daughters, the last of which Elizabeth, died in 1802. She selected as her heir, her cousin, George Cooke, requiring him in her will, to assume the name of Cooke-Yarborough. George employed Doncaster architect William Lindley around 1802 to make drawings for alterations and additions to Campsmount, some of which were adopted in later years. Around 1806, George Cooke-Yarborough commissioned sculptor John Flaxman to produce a monument to the Yarborough family, which was housed in Campsall church. When George died in 1818, Campsmount was occupied by the Cooke-Yarbroughs for over a century.

George Eustace Cooke-Yarborough, a barrister, was the last member of the family to live at Campsmount. The *Doncaster Gazette* noted on 17 January 1935 that Campsmount might be taken over by the West Riding Mental Hospitals Board and used as a mental institution; the scheme however was never carried out. The *Doncaster Gazette*, 27 August 1953, gives details of a proposed sale of Campsmount and the estate, outlining its history from the time it was vacated by the Cooke-Yarbroughs. 'Campsmount estate, which was bought by the West Riding C.C. in 1935, is to be sold by auction next month. At the outbreak of War it was requisitioned by the War Office and troops were stationed there ... Later, it was used as a hostel for European voluntary workers and other types of emergency before being derequisitioned. The Hall itself has been empty since then and the state of the premises is very poor. Anglers of the old days found the lakes at Campsmount happy hunting grounds for their pastime and very lake 'takes' of fish, especially bream, were obtained. When G.E. Cooke-Yarborough left Campsmount for Wadworth Hall [in 1930/1] he let it to Major Hibbert. Major Hibbert, commanding officer of the Kings' Own Yorkshire Light Infantry at Pontefract Barracks, stayed there until the mansion was bought by the County Council.' On 10 September 1953 the newspaper announced: 'The Hall and estate was sold to Mr John Carr for £11,000.' In subsequent years it was demolished.

Opposite above: Cantley Hall can trace its origins back to the late eighteenth century, when it was more commonly known as Cantley Lodge—H-shaped in plan, rubble rendered, three-storeys high and ten bays wide. At that time, it was owned by Childers Walbanke Childers, who transformed it into a country mansion. He was succeeded by his eldest son John, who made alterations to the house. He employed local architect William Lindley, whose influence is particularly evident in the interior, with oval-ended rooms, neatly detailed cornices, and a domed cantilever staircase.

Below: After John's death in 1812, the estate was inherited by his eldest son, also called John. From the early part of his life, John leased Cantley Hall to various tenants, including MP Michael Angelo Taylor; George Greaves and Charles Ramsden. John died aged eighty-seven years on 8 February 1886, his wife having pre-deceased him by twenty-three years, his son and heir by thirty-one years. The estate was inherited by Rowlanda Frances, John's only surviving daughter. At that time she was thirty-two and unmarried. She resided at Cantley Hall only for a while, leasing it in 1888 to a Col. Paley until around 1889. Subsequent lessees have included William Champion.

By 1894, Cantley Hall was vacant; Rowlanda returned there and starting taking an active part in church matters. During 1900, Rowlanda decided to surrender her interests in Cantley, giving instructions to London auctioneers Messrs Watton & Lee in 1901. However, the sale did not take place. Instead, Rowlanda sold the Cantley Estate to the Grasmere Company of Chesterfield.

The Hall was empty between 1898–1902 and then another succession of lessees followed. Amongst these were Douglas Vickers, and Maxim Ltd of Rotherham. In 1904, the Cantley Estate comprising 4,430 acres was sold to the Rt Hon. Earl Fitzwilliam of Wentworth Woodhouse. Under his ownership, the Hall had even more tenants including Col. John Reginald Shaw, James Peech, and Thorne brewer Thomas Darley. Under Darley's tenure, and with the Earl's permission, extensive structural alterations were carried out at the Hall. These included much demolition work, and the dining room's conversion into a modern kitchen and butler's pantry; the library became the new dining room, and the 'L-shaped drawing room was reduced, creating an extra study.

Left and above: In 1950, Earl Fitzwilliam decided to sell the Cantley Estate, which was bought by the Metropolitan Railway Country Estate. A short time after, Thomas Darley acquired the Hall from the company. In the same decade, Thomas was involved in a wrangle with Doncaster Corporation, acquiring by Compulsory Purchase Order three quarters of Cantley Park for housing. Thomas Darley died in 1982, his wife five years later. In subsequent years the Hall was occupied by motorcar dealer John Carnell, who later sold the property to Graham Kirkham, carrying out a much needed restoration programme. Cantley Hall is now a private residence and not open to the public.

Carr House, situated on a site near where the Park Hotel currently stands, in Carr House Road, was a small mansion built by mercer Hugh Childers, shortly after he purchased the Carr House estate in 1604. In that year, he also became Mayor of Doncaster. His standing in the town was confirmed again during 1611, when he was appointed Mayor of Doncaster for a second time. Hatfield (1868) states: 'Hugh Childers possessed the spirit of a gallant gentleman and was not to be thwarted in his intention.' Hugh died in 1631, his descendents, including Francis Childers, Thomas Childers and Leonard Childers. It was Leonard (b. 1673) who was associated with the famous racehorse, known either as Bay Childers or Flying Childers. Evidently, he never actually trained the horse, nor was he aware of the qualities it possessed. Before the horse gained a reputation, it was employed on mundane tasks—fetching and carrying mail from the Doncaster post office, and the exchange of letters between Carr House and Cantley Lodge, another property owned by the Childers family. Around 1719, the horse was sent to Newmarket bloodstock sales and was purchased by the Duke of Devonshire. According to Pick's *Turf Register* (1722): 'Flying Childers was allowed by sportsmen to be the fleetest horse that ever ran at Newmarket; or, as is generally believed, that was ever bred in this world.'

Opposite below: Sarah Walbanke Childers sold Carr House to J. Maw around 1805, leasing it seven years later to Peter Inchbalds who operated a school from there 1812–1817.

Right: Members of the Childers family continued to occupy Carr House until around 1750 when they moved to Cantley. The House was subsequently leased to the Marquis of Granby, who, according to William Sheardown, writing a century later, 'kept a pack of deer hounds, and hunted the neighbourhood.' The *Doncaster Gazette*, 9 September 1921, noted: 'Of the many festive doings of which old Carr House must in its time have been the scene, none was more brilliant than the entertainment given by the Marquis of Granby on 11 August 1752. Along with Viscount Downe and the Marquis of Rockingham, he had been complemented by the Corporation with the gift of the Borough Freedom, 'in a silver box gilt with gold,' and to celebrate the occasion he gave a grand banquet to the civic community at Carr House.' The photograph here depicts one of the lodges.

Above and below: For a period during the twentieth century, Carr House was a fever hospital, as noted by H.R. Wormald in *Modern Doncaster* (1973): 'The Infectious Diseases Hospital, Tickhill Road, was built 1928–1929 with new loan sanctions at a total cost of £66,348 and Carr House, which had been used temporarily for the purpose ceased to be used.' Thereafter it was deliberately destroyed by fire.

Clumber Park attracts thousands of visitors each year, predominantly from Nottinghamshire, Derbyshire, Lincolnshire and Yorkshire; some from even further afield. Originally comprising 4,000 acres, it was the last of the five great estates of the Dukeries to be established. The Clumber estate formed part of Sherwood Forest until 1707 when licence was given to John Holles, the 3rd Duke of Newcastle, to enclose it as a park for the Queen's use. It is perhaps unlikely that many of the present visitors to the park know that there was once a splendid house there, or could imagine what it looked like. The pictures reproduced here however, show the House as it once was. Clumber House was built around 1760-1770 by Stephen Wright for the Duke of Newcastle. The basic layout included four wings around a central block. Clumber Bridge, seen in one of the pictures, was built about 1770 to the designs of Stephen Wright, consisting of three, almost semi-circular arches. A large serpentine lake was constructed at a cost of over £6,000 between 1774 and 1789. Plans for alterations to the House were made in 1814, 1829 and 1856 by architects Benjamin Wyatt, Sidney Smirke and Sir Charles Barry. Only Smirke's designs, with an Italianate flavour, were actually carried out. However, in the late 1870s, fire damage caused the central part of the House to be rebuilt in the Italianate style to the designs of Charles Barry, the younger. A private chapel, for use by the Duke of Newcastle, Gothic in style, containing stained glass windows by Kempe and dedicated to St Mary, was erected in 1889. The House existed until 1937, when the 9th Duke razed the House and lakeside terraces to the ground.

Above: During the Second World War, Clumber Park was used as a munitions dump. In 1946, the park was sold by the Duke to the National Trust, now English Heritage. People presently visit the park for the peace and freedom which they find there.

58-506. Clumber Bridge   Copyright.   Scrivens.

Crookhill Hall was situated between Edlington and Clifton. It stood in the midst of ninety acres of its own park land, overlooking an extensive sweep of the countryside. The *Doncaster Gazette*, 12 June 1925, claimed that it was not a mansion around which a wealth of historic and romantic associations clung. 'Yet, it was of interest because it had been the home of one family, [the Woodyeares] for a good many years ... [So], there is not much doubt that it was a Woodyeare who built the present mansion.' Pevsner (1967) gives the following description of the Hall: 'Plain Georgian house of seven bays and two storeys with three bay pediment, quoins of even length, and a doorway with a Gibbs surround.' Colin Walton in the *Doncaster Free Press*, 3 January 1985, states: '[Crookhill Hall] consisted of a handsome entrance hall, a dining room, a breakfast room and library, and a Green Room. On the first floor were six handsome lodging rooms, with a dressing room to each, together with a water closet.' From the deeds and documents relating to the Crookhill estate held in the Doncaster M.B.C. Legal & Admin Department, details may be gleaned of how it left the Woodyeares' ownership. John Fountain Woodyeare (a retired clergyman) died in July 1880 leaving his wife Emily, the tenancy for life of the Hall. Their marriage was childless and following her death in February 1919, the estate passed to Lawrence Woodyeare Blomfield. In 1924 the Crookhill Estate was offered for sale, but was withdrawn at £3,750.

Opposite below: While Clumber House was demolished in the late 1930s, there still remains intact some interesting features within the park. These include the entrance gates, built in 1789, off the Worksop Road; Carburton Lodge; the Drayton and Normanton gates; Apley Head lodges and gate; two eighteenth-century Doric Temples designed by Stephen Wright; the Duke's study set back from the main house site; and eighteenth and nineteenth-century stables.

In 1925, Lawrence Blomfield jointly owned the estate in partnership with his son John. For a time during the 1920s, Joseph Humble was a tenant at the Hall. On 22nd March 1926, Lawrence and John sold the property to the West Riding County Council for £6,500, including the mansion, workshops, cottages and just over ninety aces of land. On 7 January 1927, the *Doncaster Gazette* gave news of developments at the Hall: 'The latest and most modern home for consumptives in the West Riding came into existence on Monday when Crookhill Hall opened its hospitable doors for the reception of early and serious consumptive cases.' The picture here shows the Hall in the early 1960s.

In 1948, on the introduction of the NHS, the Hall was inherited by the Doncaster Hospital Management Committee, continuing to run the premises as TB hospital until 1963, when it was closed, due to the decline in the incidence of the disease. Later on, the building became a target for vandals and was severely damaged by two fires in September 1968, resulting in its subsequent demolition. Later, during 1973, the grounds were converted for use as a golf course, a club-house being erected on the old Hall's site.

Conisbrough's Old Hall, in Well Gate, was once reached from Church Street or via Lady Lane/ Dark Lane (now Elm Green Lane). The Old Hall or Priory Manor, as it was also known, was where the manager of the Prior's estates lived, according to Allport in his *History of Conisbrough; From the earliest ages to the present day* (1913). He also adds: 'Like sundry other old places, it appears to have been re-built soon after the dissolution of the monasteries. Originally, it was a farmhouse, and has also been a public house [though no evidence has been found to confirm this].' Some believe the building was Conisbrough's Moot Hall, or meeting place, but local historians state that the Moot Hall was situated south of the Parish church, where the church hall now stands, and fell into such a dangerous state that it was pulled down in 1871. When the Old Hall was demolished in 1938, the *Doncaster Gazette*, from 24 November of that year said: 'Conisbrough is losing one of its oldest houses, the Old Hall, centuries old, which is now in the hands of the Housebreakers. The Old Hall is being demolished under the Conisbrough Urban District Council's slum clearance scheme and the demolition work is revealing some interesting facts of the building in the olden days.' Harry Appleyard, of Messrs Appleyard & Lumb, Conisbrough, who had the work in hand, told the newspaper that the walls of the property were about eighteen inches thick, and everywhere they went, they were being confronted with massive oak beams of which only one or two had been affected by the death-watch beetle. The porch was covered with a complete 'V' shaped piece of lead more than half an inch thick. More than four cwts of lead had been removed. It was also mentioned that the Old Hall had, for many years, been divided into three or four dwellings, and must in years gone by, judging from its substantial appearance and dignified architecture, have played an important part in the life of Conisbrough.

Allport (1913) states that the Priory/Godfrey Walker's Convalescence home, now occupied by the DMBC, is unquestionably a very old house, but contrary to the generally accepted theory, never was what its name implies, though it was closely connected with the Church. The building appears to have been the priest's house before the Conisbrough vicarage was built, and the grounds were largely used as a graveyard. In making a cellar under the House in 1868 'cart-loads' of human bones are said to have been dug up. A few years later, the entire skeleton of a woman was discovered only a few inches under the surface, close to the main entrance gate. Allport also states: 'The date when the Priory was built seems lost in antiquity; but the entire Priory Manor, or lands belonging at one time to the Priory at Lewes, came into the possession of a Mr Tudor, who rebuilt the old house and named it the Priory.' The House passed through various owners, including Godfrey Walker, 'one of the best known and most popular public men in the Don Valley.' He was senior partner in the firm of Walker & Crawshaw's Ashfield Brick works, while he was also connected with agriculture. Thereafter, his widow gave the Priory to the Sheffield General Infirmary as a convalescence home for children. Allport states: 'Most of the children come from the slums of Sheffield, and to many of the poor little things, the change must seem like a foretaste of paradise. Some Conisbrough people were displeased at the Priory being given to Sheffield, but it is questionable whether any other scheme would have done more good or have been more appreciated by those for whose benefit it was intended.' The Home was closed in December 1937. During the Second World War, the building was used for civil defence purposes. However, in recent years the property has been used as office accommodation by Conisbrough UDC and the DMBC.

The original Cusworth Hall was situated in the centre of the village and had five gables. Between 1726–1735, William Wrightson enlarged its gardens and also spent a fair amount on village improvements. Eventually, he decided upon having a larger, grander house. The new house's

foundations were dug, on a site further west to the older building in 1740, the latter being dismantled sometime later. William collaborated with Rotherham mason/architect George Platt for the new Hall's design and construction, the stone used coming from the Cusworth estate quarries in Castle Hill Wood and Raven Hill.

William's son-in-law John Battie mentioned that the central hall was 'too tall for its length'. So, Palladian-style architect James Paine was given the task of designing two wings to add to the structure. Between 1750–1755 a number of master craftsmen were involved with Cusworth Hall's alterations. Amongst these were John Watson, Joseph Rose and Francis Hayman. The total cost to build the Hall, completed around 1755, was around £20,000.

On succeeding William to the Cusworth estate in 1760, his son-in-law John Battie changed his name to Wrightson a year later, becoming known as John Battie Wrightson. John was responsible for laying out the grounds at Cusworth, calling on the services of landscape gardener Richard Woods. Even though only one hundred acres were involved, the work took five years to complete, costing many hundreds of pounds. The picture here shows Richard Heber Wrightson (1800–1891). The *Doncaster Gazette*, 1 May 1903, recalled some interesting snippets about him: 'There are of course those living who remember [him], on the back, or rather the neck, of his nag; for surely had Tod Sloan seen the gentle squire on the pigskin, Tod might have felt some jealousy of his style of riding being indulged in, and so unsportsman-like a manner.'

Successors to the Cusworth estate after John Battie Wrightson's death in 1766 included William Wrightson (1752–1827), dropping the Battie part of his surname after his twenty-first birthday; William Battie Wrightson (1790–1879); and Richard Heber Wrightson (1800–1891).

Above: Interior view of Cusworth Hall's South Tapestry Saloon.

Right: Richard Heber was succeeded in 1891 by William Henry Thomas who later took the name and arms of Battie Wrightson by Royal Licence. In 1884 he had married Isabella Cecil, the eldest daughter of the Marquis of Exeter. Initially, they lived at Warmsworth then moved in 1891 to Cusworth. The couple produced two children, Robert and Barbara, before William died at the relatively early age of forty-seven in 1903. His obituary in the *Doncaster Gazette*, 1 May 1903, mentioned: 'William Henry had spent most of his life on his estate attending personally to its most important affairs and taking a kindly interest in the welfare of his tenants and all those who were dependant upon him.'

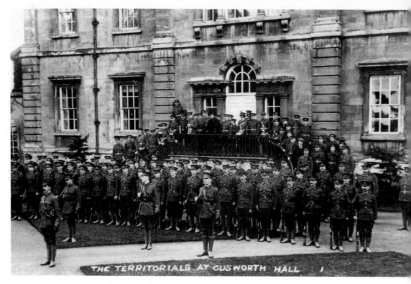

THE TERRITORIALS AT CUSWORTH HALL 1

After William's death, Lady Isabella became involved in a legal wrangle with her husband's family over the right to remain at Cusworth. However, once this was successfully overcome, she built a new dining room in 1907, behind the chapel wing to link with the kitchen corridors. Her son Robert, was the last squire at the Hall, living off the family fortune. During the Second World War, life was severely disrupted at the Hall, the grounds being utilised by the authorities as a military base. Robert Cecil and his partner Mrs Bentley did not vacate the premises and were allocated several rooms in which to live. The picture here was probably taken on 28 April 1911.

When Robert died in 1952, the Hall and estate passed to his sister Barbara who by this time was known as Mrs Maureen Pearse. To meet the heavy financial burden of Robert's death duties, assessed at around £280,000, Barbara decided to raise the sum by selling the Hall's

contents. A sale took place during October 1952 and lasted nine days. Thereafter, Barbara leased the Hall to several parties including the Ivy Mount College and the Bay Hall Timber Company Ltd, until it was purchased by the Doncaster Rural District Council in 1961 for £7,500, later to become a museum.

Doncaster's Beechfield house was built around 1812 by Henry Preston on a close or pasture ground, called Chequer or Waterdale Close. At that time, the House stood alone in a rural setting and included a dining room, drawing room, breakfast parlour, an ante-room, butler's pantry, servants' hall, housekeeper's room, larder, detached kitchen, scullery, wash house, laundry, eight bedrooms and dressing rooms, toilet, closet, servants' sleeping rooms, cellars, stabling for three horses, double coach house, hay chambers and piggery. The House stood in almost five acres, containing ornamental planting, a meadow and kitchen gardens.

By September 1829, Beechfield was owned by the Revd William Cuthbert who ran a private school on the premises. His occupation lasted another nine years until J.W. Sturgess, owner of the Bowling Ironworks, West Yorkshire, acquired the property. Two years after his death in 1861, his widow sold Beechfield to William Henry Foreman, who extended and altered the House, and also improved the gardens. He then leased the property to several tenants, amongst them being Sir Isaac Morley, Director of the Sheffield & Rotherham Railway Co.; G. Morris and Richard Morris. The latter eventually transformed the grounds at Beechfield, featuring fountains, caverns and lawns, and frequently opened them to the public.

Morris's wife continued to live at Beechfield seven years after his death in 1900, when the Trustees of W.H. Foreman's estate offered the House and adjoining lands to Doncaster Corporation for £12,500, which was accepted. In 1908, the Estates Committee recommended that the Doncaster Museum Committee be allowed to use three ground floor rooms in Beechfield for the purpose of a town museum.

On 4 November 1908, the estates committee recommended the use of some rooms on the first floor of Beechfield house for the use of art club members. During 1909, it was agreed that the sum of £150 be granted to cover the cost of removal of exhibits from the Guildhall, to and the fitting up of Beechfield, for the purpose of a museum. In the same year it was agreed that the first floor of Beechfield be known as the Municipal Art Gallery, and that a committee be formed to manage the same, consisting of four members of the art club and six members of the Corporation. Also, in 1909, Dr Corbett was appointed as curator at £50 per annum.

The art gallery opened on 28th October 1909 and Viscountess Halifax officiated at the ceremony. The remainder of the building, after conversion for museum purposes, opened to the public on 23 March 1910. A prestigious event formerly held in the art gallery was the 'Summer Exhibition'. The exhibition was staged annually between 1910-1940, except for a break from 1916 to 1921. Many artists holding national recognition were brought together at the exhibition. The above picture shows part of the grounds at the rear of the building.

At the 1931 Summer Exhibition opening, curator Norman Sylvester said that he would not apologise for the poor hanging of the pictures, as he had been shouting for a new art gallery for long enough. However, this did not occur until much later. During the Second World War the Beechfield gardens were largely taken over for growing vegetables. In the post-war years, Beechfield continued as one of the town's major institutions until the House and grounds were cleared in 1963 for the building of a new technical college.

Above and below: Doncaster's Belle Vue House, now the Grand St Leger Hotel, and featured in both pictures here, was built around 1811 on an area of land called Haigh's Close, for John Henry Maw, by Alderman Lockwood. Originally it was to be titled the Turf Hotel and was to include training stables, however it became John Henry Maw's house.

For much of the twentieth century the House was used to accommodate stable hands. In 1920, the job of caretaker of Belle Vue house was given to Jack Lindsay, and on 9 September 1937 the *Doncaster Gazette* commented: 'Do you know where the best view of the famous 'straight mile' on the Doncaster Racecourse is to be had? It is scarcely likely that you do and you cannot buy a ticket for the privilege of watching the races from this vantage point. One man has for seventeen years had almost the 'sole rights' of it. He is Mr Jack Lindsay, who since 1920 has been caretaker at Belle Vue House, which will this week be a temporary home for some five hundred stable boys ...'

The *Doncaster Civic Trust Newsletter*, July 1980, reported that the DMBC had decided to offer Belle Vue house for sale, the race committee having provided new accommodation for the stable lads. Also, as the council had no further use for the House, it was proposed to apply to the DoE for permission to demolish it. However,

the House was acquired by local builder J. Gamble who opened the premises as the Grand St Leger Hotel in 1984. Sometime afterwards the building was damaged by fire and in 1990 was taken over by the Din family, who made additions to the premises as seen here.

Eastfield House, Doncaster, formerly situated on Grandstand Road (now Leger Way) was built by John Henry Mawe around 1809 and originally intended as private speculation for a race stand. Hence the construction of its balconies and many-windowed frontage. Old prints actually show the House standing on the racecourse. Unfortunately, the building was too far out of line to be a popular 'Winning Post rendezvous' and so the balcony steps were never thronged by the visiting gentry and nobility that the owner had envisaged.

Eventually, Eastfield House became a private girls' school, run by a Miss Murphy. After her, the occupier between 1817 and 1826 was Dr Peter Inchabld, who was a rather colourful, if not eccentric character. He was an Oxford University graduate, and despite charging much higher fees than anyone else in the town (some paid over £100 per annum for his fees and 'extras') he was always in debt. After Inchbald's departure, the House was divided into two separate dwellings.

In 1828, John Rogerson from Barnsley, opened another school in the building, a classical, commercial and mathematical academy. A year later a part of the building was let to the newly established Yorkshire Institution for instruction of the deaf and dumb children, and by 1832 the institution had taken over the entire building to become the first 'home' for the present Yorkshire Residential School for the Deaf. Thereafter the building was occupied entirely by the institution. The above picture shows a scene in one of the classrooms.

In 1941, new school buildings were completed behind Eastfield House, which was conveyed to the Doncaster Corporation. During the Second World War, the old building was used by troops and ATS. Later on, it was converted into flats to relieve the post-war housing shortage. Eastfield House was demolished during late 1958 to make way for a road-widening scheme between racecourse corner and the Doncaster fire station.

Edenfield House Academy, a large house off Thorne Road, Doncaster, was built in 1832 by William Heigham. During its lifetime the Academy became the leading private school in the town and gained a wide reputation. The House was put up for auction in October 1892 and acquired by F.W. Masters for £2,500. Soon afterwards, it was demolished.

Writing in the *Doncaster Civic Trust Newsletter, 33* of March 1981, Eric Braim mentioned that Edenfield, a handsome house was built in 1894 by William Sayles Arnold, Doncaster's most successful builder, for his own occupation having acquired the land from F.W. Masters. In the 1920s and 1930s, Edenfield was regularly taken by Lord Lonsdale for Race Week, and Lord Harewood and the Princess Royal frequently stayed there as guests.

Col. John Walbanke Childers of Cantley Hall built the elegant Elmfield House around 1803. In the *Doncaster Civic Trust Newsletter*, November 1981, Eric Braim speculates that local architect William Lindley was responsible for the building's design. Furthermore, it is possible that Elmfield House was intended as a dower house for John Walbanke Childers' widowed mother Sarah. She died herself in 1817, and four years later, the House was occupied by Bradford Bolling Iron Works owner, John Sturgess, who remained there until his death in 1823.

After being tenanted by John Fountain Woodyeare of Crookhill, Elmfield House was sold in 1843 to the trustees of the estate of John Jarratt. Later on, the Jarratts leased the property to a number of tenants until 1889. After that time, the Jarratt family returned to the House which was then occupied by mining engineer John Jarratt Jarratt until his death in 1915. His daughter Ellen Charlotte Jarratt succeeded to the House and estate. Later she sold Elmfield, around 1920, to the Corporation along with around twenty-eight acres for £30,000. Thereafter, the park was developed, and unveiled near the entrance gate to the park, was the cenotaph in 1923.

Eric Braim in the *Doncaster Civic Trust Newsletter*, August 1987, criticizes the Corporation for not employing a skilled landscape designer for laying out the parkland: 'The [Corporation] Estates Committee turned to their young Estates Surveyor. He was an engineer and probably without any experience of park design. This failure to obtain skilled landscape advice has blighted the development of Elmfield Park ever since.' A feature that can be seen in the photographs reproduced here, is the dolphin fountain, created in 1925.

For a number of years it was suggested that the House could suitably accommodate an art gallery and tea-room, separate from the Beechfield Museum, but that never occurred. In the post-war year a projected new road scheme posed a threat to the tranquillity of Elmfield House and park. The road would have been 85ft wide, diverging from Bennetthorpe near the Comrades Club (formerly Elmfield Cottage), sweeping over the site of the war memorial, scything its way through Hall Cross Hill and the grounds of Elmfield House and on to join Trafford Way near the Southern bus station. That, however, never came to fruition, and in subsequent years Elmfield House has thrived as the base for a youth club and other related activities.

Thomas Aldam built the Friends' meeting house at Warmsworth in 1706. There was also an adjoining area for interments. The building was occupied by the Friends until 1798 when they converted a barn in West Laith Gate, Doncaster (seen here) for use as another meeting house, which had an adjoining burial ground. The conversion work was carried out by local builder Thomas Anelay. The west Laith Gate structure contained a caretaker's cottage and a main hall, accommodating around 200 people. In subsequent years the building was used as an adult education centre, being demolished in 1976.

High Street Buildings, Cleveland Street, Doncaster, seen here on the right, once extended from Wood Street to Young Street. They were set back from the street within gardens and once housed the clerk to the Borough Justices' Offices. The Temperance Hotel, pictured here, and existing between 1914-1921, once formed part of High Street Buildings. The premises were subsequently occupied by the Doncaster Liberal Club. After this, the buildings and gardens, which gave an almost parkland feel to the scene, were cleared and York House erected.

The most important building in the Doncaster area is arguably the Doncaster Mansion House in High Street. There are only three mansion houses in the country: at York, London and Doncaster. The purpose of the Doncaster building was to hold the mayor's banquets, balls, suppers, feasts to the judges at the assizes, and other social and public functions. Architect James Paine started work on Doncaster's mansion house or banqueting house in 1745.

The building neared completion by 1748 but at a cost considerably more than was envisaged. William Lindley added an attic storey in 1801. The reason for the attic's construction was that more space was needed and the pediment over the main building appeared very low. The omission of the pavilions from the original plan had not helped these problems. So, a decision was taken to remove the pediment, replacing it with an attic storey. The attic was intended for use by the mayor and his family, though very few mayors have actually lived in the building. It is understood that an Alderman Bentley was the last to keep up the old traditions.

Having entrusted William Lindley with previous work, the Corporation asked him to produce plans for a new banqueting hall (dining room) in 1806. This was erected to the rear of the mansion house over the arcade on the north side of the garden. Further alterations took place to the building in 1831, the Corporation having decided it was not large enough for civic entertainments. Another local

architect, William Hurst, was asked to produce plans for the improvements, which included the saloon being created by re-designing the area accommodating the old tea room and old back stairs.

The Mansion House's use has been varied. In the early days it was used as a courthouse for petty sessions and also as a concert room. Among many other notables, Liszt appeared there in 1839 and Louis Jullien, (one of the inventors of the Promenade Concert) and his unrivalled band in 1844. Also, as Doncaster was always a great racing centre, the mansion house has been the scene of many notable banquets and gatherings. In more recent times, while much finance has been spent on the mansion house's upkeep, the banqueting hall and smaller rooms have been mainly used by the DMBC for holding committee meetings. The Mansion House is pictured above whilst being re-painted.

In Doncaster during the latter half of the nineteenth century the Senior family lived in a 'Fred Flintstone' type of house, hollowed out of rock. This rock house began to emerge from within a sand-quarry in the 1850s when Pontefract-born, William Senior, set himself the task. As the land was partially excavated in the direction of Green Dyke Lane, the first section of the House emerged. The two-storey house was constructed in two stages and eventually became known by a variety of names, including Rock House, Sand House and Don Castle.

The first section of the Sand House was completed around 1857 but it is doubtful whether William Senior ever lived there, since he died in 1859. It was, however, occupied by William's son Henry Senior. In the early 1860s, Henry continued to extend the House and excavate the sand around it. The House, when completed included stables and a ballroom; the outer walls were 9ft thick and the inner walls 3ft. The House was 120ft long and 42ft wide. Window casements and door frames were fixed and the roof was covered with pantiles.

Right: Henry's next 'Sand House' project was to cut a tunnel slightly below quarry floor level, behind the east side of the quarry face. Windows cut into the side of the face allowed light into the tunnel, illuminating large magnificent sculptures, painstakingly carved by professional sculptors, in many recesses. The sculptures depicted, amongst others, the Virgin Queen, Inigo Jones and Tim Bobbin (a Lancashire poet). Henry's sculpture tunnel extended from north to south. While following a southerly direction, the tunnel turned westwards beneath Green Dyke Lane.

Below: In the late nineteenth century, the Sand House and its associated features, were a wonder of the neighbourhood and continued to be a popular place for the public to visit. When Henry Senior died in 1900, his entire estate was sold, the proceeds being divided between the immediate family. The quarry Sand House and sculpture tunnel were purchased by the Corporation. The above picture shows an interior view of the House.

Left and below: Following the Second World War the quarry from which hundreds of tons of sand had been obtained, was filled in and the Sand House area lay barren until the erection of the high-rise flats in the 1960s. Before their construction, extensive surveys were carried out to discover the full extent of the sand workings. Afterwards the sculpture tunnel and many of the passages meandering from it were back-filled and this helped to allay any fears of subsidence. These two pictures show some of the underground features.

The vicarage, standing to the north of St George's church, Doncaster. The vicarage was built in 1706 and in 1771 was noted as containing five rooms. During 1786 and 1827 it underwent improvements and enlargments, surviving until May 1932.

The *Doncaster Gazette*, 9 June 1922, described Dunscroft Abbey as: 'a whitewashed house standing well back from the road, and bearing on its plan and outline the unmistakeable stamp of the Elizabethan period.' While the building was often known locally as Dunscroft Abbey, an abbey it never was. However, the traditional name bespeaks the connection which long existed between Dunscroft, along with much of the countryside round about, and the authentic abbey of Roche, many miles away. The *Gazette* also adds: '[Dunscroft] was a 'grange'–in other words a local farm–attached to the Abbey of Roche. Other granges there were on other estates belonging to the Abbey.'

Above: The *Doncaster Gazette,* 30 March 1923, states that Edenthorpe Hall, (formerly Streetthorpe) was built somewhere about the 1770s by George Cooke-Yarbrough. Gordon Smith in the *Doncaster Gazette,* 30 June 1966, informed: 'During the late eighteenth century, Streetthorpe Hall was the residence of Lord Auckland. It was about this time that 'Edenthorpe' was adopted as a new name, 'Streetthorpe' subsequently vanished. At sometime during the Victorian period, Edenthorpe Hall was enlarged. Wide wings were added to the north and south-either side of the original eighteenth-century block.' In April 1922 the central block was gutted by fire, and subsequently demolished.

Above: Edlington Hall stood near St Peter's church in old Edlington, having a good view of the surrounding countryside. During the early eighteenth century, Samuel Buck produced a number of sketches of local country seats, Edlington Hall being one of them. Artist Mick Durrant elaborated Buck's Edlington Hall drawing, and his work is reproduced here, perhaps giving a clearer idea of how the Hall may have appeared. One of the only sources providing information about the Hall is E. Miller's *The History and Antiquities of Doncaster and its Vicinity* (1804). At the time of writing, Miller describes the Hall as being in a ruinous condition. He also mentions that from the cyphers and arms upon the ceiling of one of the rooms, it was probably built by Sir Edward Stanhope, Baronet. More recent information is provided by Magilton (1977): 'The only known [archeological] site [at Edlington] is that of Edlington Hall, south of the Church, which recent excavation in the face of current redevelopment has shown to be largely destroyed by modern burials.'

Opposite below: Edlington Rectory was formerly situated on the west side of St Peter's church. On 14 August 1969, the *Doncaster Evening Post* ran a story about a bid to save the rectory from demolition. A local businessman had bought the building some twelve months earlier hoping to restore it. After calling in a team of experts the cost was found to be too great, so he lodged an application for demolition. The rectory was on the Ministry of Housing and Local Government list of buildings scheduled as being of particular interest, and the application to pull it down annoyed several archaeological societies. A spokesman for the DRDC allegedly said: 'The building is of little historical importance and at the moment looks a shambles.' Needless to say the rectory was subsequently demolished.

The *Doncaster Chronicle*, 17 June 1881, described the Finningley estate as a most compact and important landed investment of freehold tenure, consisting of about 2,418 acres. On 21 August 1903, following the death of George Spofforth Lister Esq., JP, the late owner, the *Doncaster Gazette* noted: 'The residence contains on the ground floor, entrance hallway, bay-windowed dining room, drawing room, with small recess leading into a small conservatory, morning room, billiard room, study, housekeeper's room, butler's pantry, butler's bedroom, servants' hall, kitchen and scullery, store rooms, with dairy and boot house outside, etc. There are twenty bed and dressing rooms, stabling for fourteen horses, coach houses and well appointed out-offices.'

Later, the Finningley estate was owned by the Parker Rhodes family until the death of John Parker Rhodes in 1943. His obituary in the *Doncaster Chronicle*, 7 January 1943, said: '[He] died at Honeywick Hill, Castle Carey, Somerset last Friday. He was the only surviving son of the late Frederick Parker-Rhodes, at one time senior partner in the firm of Parker-Rhodes Cockburn and Co., solicitors of Rotherham, who lived for some years at Finningley Park. Mr Parker-Rhodes, who was educated at Uppingham and Penbroke College Cambridge, was a keen sportsman and a Fellow of the Royal Zoological Society.'

Above and below: In March 1943, the Finningley Park estate, comprising over 1,505 acres, was sold for £45,000. Starting at £15,000 and rising in bids of £1,000 and later £500, the estate was sold by auction as one lot, at the Woolpack Hotel, Doncaster to W. Elmhirst of Rotherham, who was buying on behalf of a client. The 1,505 acres included three farms, Finningley Park Hall and other lots. Six hundred acres of the estate, sold in the previous July, had realised £30,000. Pevsner (1959) wrote: 'The Georgian house of three bays and two and a half storeys now over looks a desert of sand and gravel digging.' In subsequent years, Finningley Hall was demolished.

In *Finningley* (1877), the Revd G. Harvey Woodhouse noted that in 1842 the eastern portion of the [Georgian] Rectory began to give way. He also added: 'For its restoration my own plans were simple, but I was urged forward by the expectation that a member of the [local] Harvey family was to be my successor, and a far larger house was eventually built than was really desirable.' During July 1986, Eric Braim wrote in the *Doncaster Civic Trust Newsletter No 49*: 'Our front cover is of the building which was until recently the rectory, Finningley but which ceased to be the rectory when a new one was built. This attractive Georgian building which has a large Victorian extension has recently been listed as Grade II.'

Hamilton Lodge, a villa-type residence set back from Carr House Road, was built by a Capt. Robson around 1856, to the designs of B.S. Brundell and Tom Penrice. Perhaps the lodge's most noted occupant was A.O. Edwards who developed the Wheatley Estate in the 1920s.

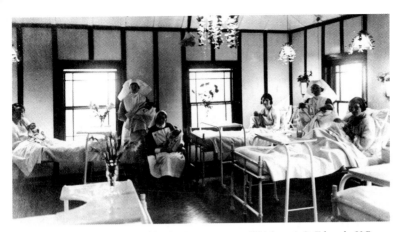

Hamilton Lodge was purchased by the Corporation in 1924 from A.O. Edwards. H.R. Wormald recorded: '[Hamilton Lodge was] developed by the Corporation as a Maternity Home at a cost between 1925 and 1928 of £6,805, also taken over by the National Health Service, has become redundant to the Service by the opening of the new Maternity Wing, in 1971, at the Royal Infirmary and is now used as a Club for Hospital Service employees in all the Doncaster Hospitals.' Since that time the premises have opened as a hotel.

Hesley Hall, containing over eighty-five rooms, is situated between Rossington and Tickhill. The *Doncaster Chronicle*, 28 November 1946, alleges that the Hall, originally a farmhouse, was extended in the 1860s, when it came into the possession of the Whitaker family, and in 1891 a chapel was opened. At one time, a private school, reputed to be the smallest in Notts for the education of tenants' children, was attached to the Hall. The children wore scarlet caps and cloaks, and were known as 'little Red Riding Hoods.' According to local legend there is a store of wine locked up in the Hall, which was hidden during the late nineteenth century and has never been traced.

One time Hesley Hall occupant, Benjamin Ingram Whitaker, born at Palermo in 1838, was a Lieutenant in the West Yorkshire Yeomanry Cavalry. Later he became a deputy Lieutenant and Justice of the Peace for Nottinghamshire and later was sheriff for the County. He died in 1922, and some details from his obituary in the *Doncaster Gazette*, 24 March 1922, include: 'Hesley Hall is a beautiful residence. An interesting feature is the museum in which Mr Whitaker was greatly interested. It contains among a large collection, the original 'Nelson' the lion from the Zoo which we believe was the model for the lions around the Nelson Monument in Trafalgar Square.'

The *Doncaster Gazette*, 10 August 1923, mentioned: '[Hesley Hall] stands amid gardens exquisitely kept and conservatories wherein bunches of bananas and grapes thrive and grow to perfection in the tropical heat. At the foot of the terraced garden is an ornamental fishpond spanned by a rustic bridge and famous for its goldfish which swim lazily beneath water lilies.'

Mrs B. Whittaker continued to occupy the Hall until her death in 1941. Thereafter, the Hall and estate passed to Maj.-Gen Sir John Whitaker, of Babworth Hall, Retford, who leased the property to the Central Council for the care of cripples, in memory of Lady Pamela Whitaker. It was occupied by that organization until 1973. The property is presently occupied by the Hesley Group of Schools who took control in the mid-1970s.

According to Miller (1804): 'In the year 1673, Hickleton Hall belonged to Sir John Jackson, Baronet.' Afterwards, it came into the hands of Godfrey Wentworth. He built a new mansion there around 1730, pleasantly situated, and commanding a very extensive prospect to the west. Additions to the Hall were made about 1775. According to Pevsner (1959) the stables at Hickleton Hall date from around 1750, the Gate Lodge around 1910, in the style of Lutyens. At the same time the statues were installed in the garden.

Magilton (1977) states: 'The surviving [Hickleton] estate wall, incorporating stone mullioned windows, running along the south side of the village street is well worth preserving, and appears to include part of the earlier hall designed by Smythson (?) Hickleton Hall itself [is] a mid-eighteenth century structure.'

Mention was made in the *Doncaster Chronicle*, 10 June 1932, of the copious supplies of the famous home-brewed Hickleton ale which Lord Halifax himself took daily at luncheon, and to which he attributed much of his good health. 'The ale is brewed on the estate, and the recipe for it is a closely guarded secret.' However, by 1935, Lord Halifax's association with Hickleton was lessening. He donated a number of the Hall's pictures to Temple Newsam House, formerly the family home until sold to Leeds City Council in 1904.

In the late 1940s, Hickleton Hall was acquired by the Sisters of the Order of the Holy Paraclete, an Anglo-Catholic sisterhood, who used it as a boarding and day school for girls until 1960. A year later, the Hall was taken over as a Sue Ryder Home for European stateless persons. The Hall currently accommodates a nursing home.

Pevsner (1959) suggests that the central tower of High Melton Hall dates from the medieval period yet the main section was built around 1757, with a wing being added in 1878. The centre of the building is three storeys high, the wings two storeys. The Hall and estate was formerly occupied by the Fountayne, Montagu and Lindley Wood families. During the eighteenth century John Fountayne was formerly the Dean of York.

During the twentieth century, High Melton Hall was the scene of a robbery. In 1908, eighteen year old Percy Finn, a second footman at the Hall, stole a tiara, the property of Mrs Montagu, wife of F.J.O. Montagu, and then tried to obtain £500 from her for its safe return. Unfortunately for Finn, he left a trail of clues, which eventually resulted in the police arresting him.

In 1926, Melton and Barnburgh Halls were purchased from Capt. F.J.O. Montagu through private treaty by Messrs G.W. Meanley & Sons, Mexborough builders and contractors. The greatest changes were made in the late 1940s when more than £200,000 was spent on High Melton Hall and it was converted into a teacher training college, a new residential block being built in the grounds.

The *Doncaster Chronicle*, 1 July 1954, stated that High Melton Hall, the country home, is now a building for people who want to learn. It also talked of the Hall ghost: 'It is reputed to appear in one of the rooms in the old tower, where the walls are so thick that wardrobes and bookshelves have been built into them.'

Hooton Pagnell is the old seat of the Norman family of Paganel, lords of Leeds, but it has been occupied for a number of years by the Wardes. Although surrounded by industrial villages, the area remains untouched, surviving with a rural splendour, the Hall itself offering an uninterrupted view of a broad sweep of country reaching up to the Pennines.

E.1.3 L9-19. The Hall, Hooton Pagnell.

Ralph de Paganel built the oldest part of Hooton Pagnell Hall as a hunting box (lodge) and additions were made to it by his successors until it developed into the embattled Manor House which is visible today. The *Doncaster Gazette*, 1 October 1926, states: '[The Hall] was entirely remodelled in the latter part of the eighteenth century ... The earliest part of it was undoubtedly the western wing in front of the gateway ... There was [probably] nothing left of the old Norman house of Ralph Paganel, which was perhaps a small house. Nothing was known about that kind of house. But, about the beginning of the 14th century, there seemed to have been a good deal of building going on and much of it was rebuilt in the latter part of the 18th century. A wing was added and later on the whole house seems to have been refaced. At another time much of it was replastered.'

Left: The *Doncaster Gazette*, 7 September 1959, tells a tale of the Hall's ancient gateway: '... the justices who resided at Hooton Pagnell Hall had their own prison chamber for the detention or punishment of criminals. It is on the first floor of the picturesque and ancient gateway which leads into the courtyard ... the hole in the roof was probably used for the lowering of food and water to the prisoners.'

Whilst Hooton Pagnell is regarded as the quietest and most picturesque village in the DMBC area, there were certain indiscretions taking place amongst the estate workers during the 1890s, prompting Julia Ward Aldam to lead her own moral crusade. In 1894 she wrote them a letter, parts of which are included here:

'Dear Sir or Madam
It is with the greatest pain I have to send this circular letter to all my tenants in the Parish of Hooton Pagnell in consequence of the lamentable state of the morals of that place. But I felt it my bounden duty to make the following rules, viz: That any member of the family of any of my tenants having an illegitimate child or children born to them or being proved to be the father of such child or children in the parish of Hooton Pagnell shall at once receive notice to quit, such notice to take effect at an early a date as possible ...'

In more recent times, the Hooton Pagnell estate and Hall have fallen to the Warde Norburys'. The Hall is presently the private residence of Anthony Warde Norbury and is not open to the public.

St Chad's Hostel, having the appearance of a modern house, contrasting with other village architecture, was established at Hooton Pagnell in 1904 as a preparatory centre for the training of candidates for holy orders. It was an offshoot of St Chad's College at Durham University and after a year spent at Hooton Pagnell the students proceeded to Durham and took their degrees. At the outbreak of hostilities in 1914, the numbers began to dwindle, many of the students joining the army as chaplains, combatant officers, or private soldiers. The Warde-Adams had allowed the use of the hostel building, rent-free. The old fashioned, well-timbered hostel buildings are now used as village hall and club.

Hooton Pagnell Vicarage, a mock Jacobean building dating from around 1850, though Magilton (1977) suggests the core may be earlier.

Right and below: Kirk Bramwith Rectory, constructed during the mid-nineteenth century, has mullioned sash windows and hood mouldings. It is topped by a steep Welsh slate roof with stone coped gables. Magilton (1977) noted: '[A] limestone font in the rectory garden.'

Above: Lindholme is a tiny village near Hatfield Woodhouse, consisting of a few houses and a Hall, once the property of Lord Allerton. The Hall was formerly in the centre of a large game preserve and was remarkable for the wealth of romance which has been woven about the hermit who is supposed to have lived there some 300 years ago. There was a large sale on the premises in 1911, which included valuable household furniture and effects. The *Doncaster Chronicle*, 19 January 1933, noted: 'The yellow crinkly track which drags itself painfully over two miles of moorland to Lindholme Hall, is a road of enchantment. The ancient Hall which it eventually reaches, is owned by Lord Allerton and is used as a farmhouse, a dear old building where legends and strange stories foregather; a land teeming with fur and feather, a land of great uncanny silences.' The article quoted a story about one of the Hall's many legends, Billy Lindholme: 'Billy Lindholme stretched his nine feet of vigorous manhood, and rose quickly from his long bed in Lindholme Hall. The giant hermit had uprooted a score of birch trees, and already he was beginning to clear a rough track through the forest. 'Devil help me' he growled as he stopped to wipe the sweat from his gigantic brow. And, dancing wildly through the woodlands, came the Devil himself ... they formed an unholy compact ... Moorland debris was hurled into the eerie lake by the Hall, and the beasts of the field and the birds of the air raced through the bracken. And in this unholy marriage they say, Billy the nine foot hermit of Lindholme and the Devil built the road through the forest. That road, overgrown with bracken and curtained by birch trees, can still be seen.' In recent years the Hall has been occupied by the Lyons family.

Opposite above: Loversall Hall is T-shaped, constructed of limestone ashlars, and appears to have been built in 1811. The servants' wing, built of coursed limestone rubble and attached to the rear of the main block, seems to be contemporary. There has been no suggestion from either external or internal examinations that the present building incorporates part of an earlier hall on the same site. The kitchen garden is held to be the site of the previous Hall, and buried foundations are said to occupy much of the area. A dovecote in the north-east corner of the garden dates from the late sixteenth to seventeenth century and probably accompanied the previous Hall.

4. Loversall Hall. Doncaster. J.S.&S.

Below: Patricia Seddon in *Loversall* (1972) gives more details of the old Hall and the building of the new one: 'George Augustus was the last occupant of the old Hall ... [he and his wife] came to Loversall, but he died suddenly, 5 May 1808 aged twenty-eight. In 1808, the demolition of the old Loversall Hall began. The new Hall took three years to build for [James] Fenton took up residence in 1811 and remained until 1816.'

James Fenton was fifty-six at the time of the new Hall's construction. Patricia Seddon says it is not known who designed or built Loversall Hall and what expenses were incurred. It is also unclear why James Fenton settled at Loversall, having to leave after only five years due to financial difficulties. The next occupant was his son William Carr, who took an alternative surname to honour his grandmother. William remained at Loversall until his death in 1855. The Hall's subsequent inhabitants included the Revd Alexander Cooke until 1849, and Francis Huntsman until 1879. Thereafter, the Hall was leased to H. Phelps Pope and his brother John, until the latter's death in January 1894.

Auxiliary Hospital. Loversal Hall. Doncaster. 5th July. 1916.

The Hall then passed to Sophia Flora Cooke Yarborough, who moved there with her husband Lt-Col. Gray Townshend Skipwith. The latter died in 1900 and was succeeded to the Loversall estate by his son Capt. C.G.Y. Skipwith. After retiring from the army, he took up farming at Loversall and was an active public worker. During the First World War, Loversall Hall was used as a hospital. It was closed on 14 February 1919, having treated in all, 1,784 patients. The House was loaned for that purpose by Mrs Skipwith, who took personal charge.

Sophia Skipwith died in 1940. During the Second World War, the Skipwiths and Loversall Hall played their part in the war effort, just as they had done earlier in the century. Capt. C.G.Y. Skipwith died at Loversall in 1967 aged seventy-six, his wife deciding to sell the Hall and estate a year later. A.E. Harrison bought the Hall and it has passed through various owners since that time, including Malcolm Colbear who used the premises as offices, one of which is seen above.

Nether Hall was formerly at the centre of a thirty acre woodland park until just over a century ago, the estate being developed for housing. Information in the *Doncaster Gazette*, 18 October 1973, informs: 'The present Hall was probably erected between 1671 and 1723, the style and shape of its windows suggesting it was built about 1690.' The *Gazette*, 28 March 1935, gives details of an earlier structure and slightly contradicts the above information: 'The original building was erected in 1461, and there were some further alterations about 1760 ... some panelling [recently taken down, revealed] a scrawled message in thick black pencil 'alterations by Samuel Sykes, 1811.' Arguably, Robert Copley was the Hall's most significant owner, the Hall first coming into the Copley family's possession in 1487.

Robert Copley was visited by clergy, scientists, poets and musicians, amongst them were: William Herschel, the Astronomer Royal; Gray the poet, and his friend and biographer, Mason. Robert also added a double-storeyed music room to the Hall. After his death in 1723, the estate descended to various individuals including Thomas Newby Copley, the Hon. Mrs Cochane and J.F. Tempest.

According to the *Doncaster Gazette*, 21 May 1920, the Copley estate passed into other hands by public sale during December 1855. The chief purchaser was William Henry Foreman upon whose death in 1869 the property passed to Maj. Alexander Browne. Previously, in the years between 1861 and 1879, the Hall was opened as a school by George Hardy. On 4 March 1881, it was learned that Nether Hall had been purchased by a Mr Wilson for building purposes and would be laid out in suitable building plots by Messrs Wilson and Masters. Doncaster builder Henry Flowitt was also involved, and made a vain attempt to turn Nether Hall into a pub. On 7 September 1906 the Doncaster Gazette informed: 'Old Nether Hall is in the hands of the repairers prior to being taken over by Lord Scarbrough, on behalf of the Queen's Own Yorkshire Dragoons Imperial Yeomanry, as the headquarters of the Regiment.'

On 2 May 1920 it was reported: 'The Doncaster Rural District Council and Board of Guardians are negotiating for the purchase of Nether Hall, at present in the occupation of the West Riding Territorial Association and used as the headquarters of the Yorkshire Dragoons and of the 3rd West Riding Infantry Brigade (T.F.), and as a recruiting office.' By January the following year, the transaction had been completed. In 1935, alterations took place in Nether Hall: 'electric light is being installed, and light oak panelling in modern style is taking the place of the dark old wood of bygone years.' The picture here is believed to show Mrs Flowitt.

Workmen stumbled on many queer secrets that the old Hall had guarded closely for many years, including a large bath, allegedly used by a man weighing twenty-two stones. During the 1980s, the building was altered to provide more office accommodation for the DMBC Finance Department. In particular, the former committee room and the former music room, which had been converted into a council chamber for the DRDC were altered to enable the rooms to be used as offices.

Pevsner (1958) states that Owston Hall, erected by Col. Bryan Cooke, was designed by William Porden. 'It is a simple late-eighteenth-century house of two storeys with three bay pediment on giant Ionic pilasters. [The] entrance hall opening, as usual, through a screen of two columns towards a spacious staircase [is] lit by a Venetian window.' However, while Porden prepared some designs for Owston, these were never carried out. Instead, William Lindley undertook additions and alterations at Owston in 1794.

For many years, the Owston Hall and estate was owned by successive generations of the Davies-Cooke family, tracing their descent from Henry Cooke, second son of Henry Cooke, 2nd Baronet of Wheatley. He purchased the lands of Owston from the family of Adams and became seated there about 1700.

The *Doncaster Chronicle*, 1 July 1937, carried a story about Philip Davies-Cooke being one of the first private persons in this country to import a zebra. A cart was specially made for the zebra to pull. Earlier, on 23 May 1913, the newspaper had reported: 'for the past three years the Hall has only been occasionally occupied, when the owner P.B. Davies Cooke comes over from his seat in Wales to make a short stay.' A list of former tenants was then conveniently provided: 'Mr Mathews, a well-known Sheffield business gentleman, was the last to live there from 1905 to 1910. Before him was Mr C.E. Charlesworth, the well-known colliery owner, from 1897 to 1903, and before him Mr R. Ripley, a wealthy Bradford dyer, from 1886 to 1896.'

Under the heading 'Hall's New Role' the *Doncaster Chronicle*, 14 March 1935, announced a dramatic development: 'Owston Hall, the home of the Davies-Cooke family for centuries, has now been converted into flats.' In spite of several changes of use during the twentieth century, Owston Hall still survives today.

View of the vicarage, Owston.

Rossington Bridge House, formerly a coaching inn on the Great North Road and a pub called the Doncaster Arms or Corporation Arms. It formed part of Doncaster Corporation's Rossington Estate. References to the House holding a license can be traced back to 1760, though the present building dates from around 1789.

Rossington Bridge House continued to be used as an inn until 1850, when the licence was not renewed. Tom Bradley in *The Old Coaching Days in Yorkshire* (1889) mentions: 'A few of the coaches were horsed from the Rossington Bridge Inn, and the stages they worked were from Rossington Bridge to Barnby Moor on the one hand and Red House on the other.' From 1850, the property remained primarily a private house. One of its noted tenants during the twentieth century was P.H. Beales, consultant ear, nose and throat surgeon at Doncaster Infirmary.

On 11 May 1939 the *Doncaster Chronicle* reported: 'Farm buildings at Rossington Bridge, at the junction of Sheep Bridge Lane and the Great North Road, are to be demolished and in their place is to be erected a new hotel.' However, the pub was never built. Yet, during the late 1990s, Rossington Bridge House returned to being a pub, becoming the Frog and Parrot.

A mansion named Shooter's Hill formerly existed on the site of the present Rossington Hall. The old house was erected by James Stovin around 1773, on land leased from Doncaster Corporation, who were Lords of the Manor. With the passing of the Municipal Corporation Act of 1835, the Corporation's financial deficit was such that the Rossington Estates were sold in 1838, the highest bid being made by Leeds' Woollen manufacturer, James Brown.

James Brown subsequently renamed the house as Rossington Hall, employing architect W.M. Teulon during the 1860s, to carry out alterations. In the following decade, Shooter's Hill was destroyed by fire, and the present Hall was built to the designs of Teulon in the early 1880s. The work was supervised by R.J. Streatfield, who inherited the Rossington properties from his uncle James Brown Jnr, in 1877 after his death. R.J. Streatfield, died in 1931, and Rossington Hall and estates then passed to Miss Annette Streatfield. On her death in 1937, the Hall and estates were inherited by James Rowland Scarlett. In the following year, the Hall and estates were put up for sale

Right: The Hall was eventually sold to a Roman Catholic community known as the White Fathers. Frank Clarke in his *Rossington: glimpses into past* (1986) gives details of ghostly sightings at the Hall. 'One relates to a liveried footman who was seen bearing a tray ... Another concerns a member of the Royal Veterinary Corps stationed at the Hall during the Second World War and who is said to have seen an old gentleman in frock coat and tall hat, walking unsteadily with the aid of two sticks, following one of his comrades as he patrolled the stables.' The picture opposite shows James Brown Jnr.

Below: In 1949, one hundred and eleven years after it had been sold, the Rossington estate, albeit much smaller, and the Hall, returned to the Corporation's keeping. Within the confines of the Hall a special school was established in 1953. During 1984, the Hall's stable block was occupied by the South Yorkshire Apprentice Racing Training School. The above picture shows an interior view of the Hall.

William Lindley designed Rossington Rectory/Amethyst House for use as a schoolhouse and schoolroom. It was built in 1801, but three years later Lindley altered his designs and the structure was converted for use as a rectory. For many years after, it was occupied by countless incumbents of the Church of England Living. However, in 1979 the Sheffield Diocese decided to sell it.

Rossington Rectory was subsequently purchased by local businessman, Ahmed Shah. His son Nadeem converted the building into a nursing home in 1987. Around 1990, a massive extension was added to the original rectory building. Nadeem Shah then sold the property in 1995, though it still remains a nursing home.

The first recorded house at Sandbeck was built around 1626, by Sir Nicholas Saunderson. His family was succeeded by the Lumleys in 1724. Thomas Lumley was a younger son of the 1st Earl of Scarborough, becoming 3rd Earl of Scarborough, his elder brother predeceasing him. Plans survive from this time for remodelling the House but were never carried out. Thomas died in 1752, and his son and heir married, in the same year to Barbara Savile, living at Glentworth.

In 1753, Thomas and Barbara engaged James Paine to produce plans for altering Glentworth, but these were never carried out. Preferring to live at Sandbeck, they decided to move there. James Paine was first called to Sandbeck in 1757, making a number of drawings for a variety of the Earl's building plans. Eventually, Paine produced ideas to make alterations and additions to the old house, and other records suggest that the House was remodelled rather than rebuilt.

One of the main features of the old House, sometime known as the salon, was adapted to a ballroom. The room contains one of the finest ceilings in this part of the country. The design of the 'new' house has often been described as a great achievement by Paine, exploiting to good effect the difficulties of adding to another building. The remodelling work was done using stone from the nearby Roche Abbey quarry. Around the time of the alterations, Capability Brown was called upon to make a lake at Sandbeck. The picture here shows the stables at Sandbeck.

During the early nineteenth century, a Doric portico, seen in one of the pictures, was added to the building. Today, Sandbeck still belongs to the Scarboroughs, but is not open to the public.

Scawsby Hall was sold as part of the Sprotbrough estate in 1925, and described as a fine old house suitable for a gentleman's occupation. Magilton (1977) noted that it was around a seventeenth-century cement rendered limestone building, 'with a few surviving mullions.'

The original Scrooby Manor House, also noted as Archbishop's Palace, was probably built in the twelfth century. The manor house would have been well situated as a hunting lodge, being close to the Hatfield Chace and Sherwood borders. By the early seventeenth century, William Brewster Jnr, was holding meetings of the Scrooby Separatist church in there. Having been allowed to fall into disrepair by the mid-seventeenth century, 'the dilapidated manor house and its outbuildings were demolished following a demolition order granted by Charles I,' according to M. Dolby in *Scrooby* (1991). He also adds that part of one wing of the manor house survived, and around 1750 it was renovated as a farmhouse for the Archbishop's tenant. It is that building which can still be seen today.

Serlby Hall is hidden amongst wooded parkland, two miles south of Bawtry, between Scrooby and Ranskill. It was built in 1740 for John Monkton, the 1st Viscount of Galway. Eminent Palladian architect, James Paine, designed the building, though it was considerably altered in 1812 by local architects Lindley and Woodhead, and little of the former's work is evident in the interior. The two wings, which were a prominent feature in Paine's original designs were demolished.

The Hall remained in the ownership of the Galway family throughout the nineteenth century and in 1911 the 7th Viscount Galway made further alterations to the House. In later years the Hall's contents were sold, and the Galways relinquished ownership of the property. In 1980, the House was bought by Maj. Geoffrey Berry. However, a little later, the Royal Trust Bank repossessed the House. The buyer was a local businessman who, since that time, has undertaken a major restoration programme on the property.

The *Doncaster Chronicle*, 29 April 1932, mentions that the Hall was 'built about 1600 [and] has always remained in the Nevile family.' It was added: 'Skelbooke Hall has not one ghost, but many. It seems to shelter ghosts ...' On 2 November 1950 the same newspaper was reporting that the link with the Nevile family had been severed. Maj. P.M. Nevile had sold the house to A.L. Metcalf, a Midlands businessman. The *Chronicle* also added: 'There are ten bedrooms, two entrance lodges, garages, paddock and stabling ...There is a magnificent Blue Room with a priests refuge used by persecuted monks from Hampole Priory.'

Skellow Grange was originally called Newsome Grange and externally stuccoed. Miller (1804) said Skellow Grange was the pleasant seat of Godfrey Higgins, Esq., adding: 'The mansion was built by his father, with this disadvantage, that a piece of land which extended within two or three yards of the south front of the House, belonged to the late George Ann, Esq. of Burghwallis. However, a short time before his death, Mr Higgins fortunately purchased off him not only this land, but also the manor of Skellow.'

Godfrey Higgins' obituary in the *Doncaster Gazette*, 14 June 1861, mentions: 'Three generations of the family of Higgins have resided at Skellow Grange, the first purchase in the parish having been made by them in 1770 of John Killingbeck, of Clayton. The House has been much improved and the estate undergone considerable change ... Skellow Grange and the estate will, we hear, go to Mrs Hatfield, wife of the late Mr Hatfield, of Thorp Arch, near Tadcaster.'

In later years the Grange was occupied by racehorse owner W.H. Humble, and latterly by a Mr Turnbull. On 2 July 1964 the *Doncaster Gazette* carried a story headed 'Future of Skellow Grange in balance' noting: 'It was recently sold and on Saturday, members of DRDC were told that the new owner [Mr Turnbull] had applied for permission to demolish it and replace it with a new building. It was decided that the Council should inspect the Grange to decide whether or not it is worth preserving for its historical value.' Skellow Grange was subsequently demolished.

In the grounds of Skellow Grange.

Magilton (1977) mentions that Skellow Hall and out-buildings, possibly dating from the seventeenth century, are of coursed rubble, some with pantile roofs and slabbed eaves, triangular vents and coped gables. On 21 July 1949, the *Doncaster Chronicle* wrote that Skellow Hall, former home of Capt. R.C. Davies Cooke, a Doncaster magistrate, was to be equipped for use as a children's home at a cost of £4,000. The building survives today.

South Belmont (later known as The Lodge), a small villa type of residence off South Parade, was built around 1813 by William Haigh, a school teacher and later agent for Lord Fitzwilliam's Irish estates. Mrs Franks, sister of the Revd Franks of Campsall, occupied South Belmont for a number of years until her death in 1843. For a time after that, several daughters of banker Leonard Walbanke Childers lived at South Belmont. However, in 1890, A.J. Bethel bought the property and changed its name to 'the Lodge'. In 1890, local architect J.G. Walker, produced plans for the building of stables and a coach house at the Lodge.

The *Doncaster Gazette*, 23 July 1926, recorded: 'The well-known residence, known as The Lodge, South Parade, Doncaster, has been acquired by the Doncaster Collieries Association, who will remove their offices there from Hall Gate, after some necessary alterations have been made ... The last occupant of The Lodge was the late Councillor Franks, upon whose death it changed hands. Before him, it was the home for a number of years of the late ex-councillor Patrick Stirling. During Councillor Franks' ownership, it was let on more than one occasion to the Earl of Lonsdale for Race Week.' The Lodge remained with the NCB until recent times, subsequently being acquired as offices by Nabarro Nathanson.

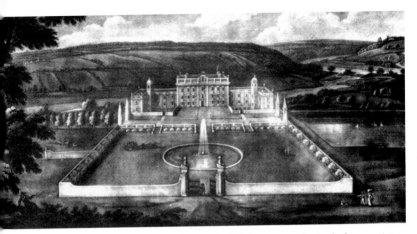

Sir Godfrey Copley built Sprotbrough Hall around 1685, his ancestors having had connections with the estate from 1516. The Hall, probably replacing an older house which had existed nearer the church, sat comfortably amidst formal gardens in the Dutch and French style, commanding a wide view of the surrounding countryside.

Gordon Smith, in *Sprotbrough Hall* (undated) states: 'Sprotbrough Hall was built of local limestone and externally stuccoed and quoined. The central block was three storeys in height, headed with a high blocking course and a balustered parapet above. This 'original' block was seven bays wide (sash windows) and had a centre doorway surmounted by a segmental pediment.'

Apart from politics, Sir Godfrey Copley also found time to pursue his interest in hydrostatics, constructing a magnificent ornamental fountain in the Sprotbrough Hall's grounds, around 1703. This came about following a visit to the Duke of Devonshire's Chatsworth House. Sir Godfrey Copley died of quinsy in 1709, his son was already dead, so Sprotbrough passed to Lionel Copley of Wadworth. Thereafter followed a succession of Copleys, and though failures in the direct line occurred, relatives were always found to succeed, taking the family name in lieu of their own.

The Copley's Sprotbrough reign finally came to an end following a strange sequence of events during the early 1920s. Under the headline 'Death Separates, and Re-unties. Sprotbrough Squire and Lady Die within four Days,' the *Doncaster Gazette*, 29 June 1923, reported the deaths at the Hall of Brigadier-General Sir Alington Bewicke Copley, and his wife Lady Bewicke Copley (Baroness Cromwell). Their son Robert Godfrey Wolsely Bewicke-Copley took control of the Hall and estate, but this was short lived, as the property was subsequently sold to meet heavy death duties, incurred following the death of his parents.

The Hall's contents were sold in February 1926, and by mid-April the *Doncaster Gazette* was reporting: 'The demolition of Sprotbrough Hall is well under way.' Gordon Smith offers a final comment on the Hall's demise: 'The idea that Sprotbrough Hall was shipped to the United States is completely wrong ... the shell of the House was brought down by hand, and buried in the basement to level the ground. All remaining masonry was taken to lay the foundation of Brompton Road, then being built in the park.'

The Sprotbrough Rectory is thought to date back approximately 400 years. In the 1840s it was drastically altered, but not rebuilt as previously assumed. The rectory paddock was sold in the early 1960s. Orchard school is presently on the site. The rectory mews estate was sold in 1983 to builders. In the same year, Trevor Miller purchased the rectory from the church and saved it from demolition. A theory put forward, is that the rectory is the original Sprotbrough Hall, and that the owners had the new Sprotbrough Hall built, selling or giving up the old Hall to the church.

Thorne Hall, a pebble-dashed, three-storey building with a Welsh slate roof and central pediment, was erected around the mid-eighteenth century. An earlier Hall had existed on a different site, once providing a home for Cornelius Vermuyden. The new Thorne Hall was largely associated with the Ellison family, and Henry Ellison appears to have been the last resident of this family in the 1820s. Later occupants included Makin Durham, and F.D. Foster. During the First World War, the Hall served as a preparatory school, and was closed for a time. Later on it was purchased by Thorne RDC.

Tickhill Castle is owned by Her Majesty the Queen, in right of her Duchy of Lancaster. It has been claimed that Roger de Buisli, a close friend of William the Conqueror, built the earthworks and constructed the wooden fortifications, which later became known as Tickhill Castle. The motte-and-bailey type castles were some of the earliest built by the Normans, and Tickhill is a good example. The gatehouse, clearly visible from the road and possibly dating from the 1100s, contains some of the earliest stonework to be found within the area.

Following the civil war, the castle keep and domestic buildings were demolished. John Leyland visited 'Tickhil' noting that 'All the buildinges withyn the (Castle) area be down, saving an old haulle.' The Hall may have stood against the wall just south of the gatehouse. A roof mark of the gable end can be seen on the bailey wall. The Hall may just have been a barn and it is most likely that it stood on a site now occupied by the house. The latter was probably built by the Hansby family towards the end of the sixteenth or early seventeenth century.

West of Tickhill Castle in 1260, an Augustinian Friary was established by the Clarel family, living in Clarel Hall in Westgate. Tom Beastall in his *Tickhill Portrait of an English Country Town* (1995) mentions: 'John Clarel chaplain to the Pope granted the foundation to the Austin Friars in return for their intercession for the souls of himself and his family and that of Sir John Mancell formerly treasurer of York.' By the fourteenth century, around twenty-four friars lived at the friary. Yet, by the dissolution of the monasteries in 1538, the numbers had waned to around eight.

The present Friary, according to Magilton (1977) is, 'a former barn with a date stone of 1653 in the street gable end.' The House also contains a thirteenth-century lancet window and other masonry from the original friary. There is also a thirteenth-century archway with dog's tooth decoration in the garden.

Rock House at Tickhill Spital, now converted to a nursing home. Magilton (1977) noted: 'Presumed medieval hospital site at crossroads. Human skeleton was found at Rock House [1972] and may have formed part of cemetery.'

Gordon Smith (1990) mentions: 'John Battie I (1616–1676) of Wadworth, purchased the Manor of Warmsworth in 1668. Shortly afterwards he must have partly rebuilt the manor house, because the hearth tax registers for 1664 and 1672 reveal that the property had twelve hearths, whereas as in a register compiled eight years earlier, it only had eight. His son, John Battie II (1663–1724) carried out a complete rebuilding of the house during the early eighteenth century. This is borne out by Ralph Thoresby, the Leeds antiquary and diarist, who after a visit to Warmsworth in 1703, mentions in his diary: 'the new house which is very pretty for the size but scarcely finished.'

The *Doncaster Chronicle*, 8 March 1945, notes the continued existence of part of the earlier building: 'The Hall was built in 1702 with the exception of the east wing, which was standing in the time of Henry VIII.' John Battie II married Isabella Wrightson (daughter of William Wrightson, builder of Cusworth Hall) in 1748. John inherited the Cusworth Estate in 1760, changing his name to John Battie Wrightson. Warmsworth Hall, thus became part of the Cusworth

Estate, and a succession of tenants appear to have occupied the property, perhaps the most noted was Col. Anthony St Leger, during the late eighteenth century.

According to David Morgan Rees in *Warmsworth Hall*, undated: 'there is a strong possibility that the origin, of the famous Doncaster horse race, the St Leger may be connected with Warmsworth Hall.'

Other Warmsworth Hall tenants have included Samuel Clowes, a Major in the Volunteers; Francis Ottley Edmunds; Richard Heber Wrightson, son of William Wrightson of Cusworth; Lady Charlotte Fitzwilliam, sister of Earl Fitzwilliam; William Henry Thomas (later Battie-Wrightson); and Col. Heydeman, a German-born Bradford mill owner. W. H. Battie-Wrightson, lived at Warmsworth Hall until 1891, when he moved with his family to Cusworth Hall.

In 1945, Robert Cecil Battie-Wrightson sold a proportion of his Warmsworth estate, including Warmsworth Hall for £2,500 to Ernest Roper of Sheffield. The Hall was subsequently occupied by local optician, J.R. Hebditch. During the latter's tenure, a section of the building on the east side, formerly used as a banqueting hall and said to have been part of an earlier house, was demolished due to its poor condition. Between the early 1960s and the mid-1980s the Hall, along with a group of newly erected adjoining buildings, formed the site for British Ropes' new head offices. Presently, the Hall forms part of the Moat House group of hotels. The aerial view shows British Ropes' extension to the Hall.

Thomas Aldam built the Quaker meeting house at Warmsworth in 1706. It was occupied by the Friends until 1798 when they converted a barn in West Laith Gate, Doncaster, for use as another meeting house. The Warmsworth structure was not used until 1912, when it was restored to the Friends by W.W. Warde Aldam. By 1947, the meeting house was being used by Warmsworth over-60s club, lasting until recent years, before being converted to a private house.

Warmsworth Parsonage House/Rectory was enlarged and altered by the Revd Charles Edward Thomas around 1861. The Revd Thomas, was one of the most noted Warmsworth rectors, holding the position of rector for nearly thirty years, before moving to Hemsworth where he died in 1901. Warmsworth Rectory was improved on several occasions throughout the twentieth century, before being converted in to flats during the 1970s, and being subsequently demolished. A new, smaller rectory was eventually built on an adjacent site.

The White House Warmsworth, demolished during the construction of the A1 motorway developments in the early 1960s.

Green House (or the Cumberland Hotel) stands on an area formerly called Lousy Bush Close. For many years the property was used as a farmhouse and was sometimes known as the Bowling Green House. Amongst the former residents was Dr E. Chorley, Mayor of Doncaster, 1821. During the twentieth century, the House was bought by Messrs Tennant Bros, Brewers of Sheffield around 1940. The intention then was to build a large residential hotel, but the War prevented a start being made. The Green House Hotel opened in 1951. Over its years in existence as a pub, the name was changed to the Cumberland.

A description of the former site of Wheatley Hall appeared in the company magazine *International Harvester Round*, Autumn 1966. 'Wheatley Hall was situated in a position roughly corresponding to the site of the present Implement Sales Warehouse, at the extreme western end of the Doncaster International Harvester complex. There were farm buildings where the King George Hotel now stands, and the gamekeeper's and blacksmith's cottages

were on the present site of ICI Fibres Ltd. Other farm buildings occupied the land which now houses Bingham and Sons ...'

Wheatley Hall, built in 1683 by Sir Henry Cook Bart, was a solid looking, many windowed building of four storeys, one of which was below ground level. The architecture was characteristic of that period, displaying much fine and well-proportioned stone work, with a profusion of windows; and internally it possessed some of the best woodwork in the country. To the south, was a lawn ornamented with some fine trees. The park extended over one hundred and three acres. The mansion was in close proximity to the river Don. It was said that the site of Wheatley Hall was by no means the best that could have been chosen on the estate for the mansion, the fair outlook from which was often impaired and rendered dreary when the Don overflowed its banks, which was pretty frequently.

The Hall was the seat of the Cooke family until the early years of the twentieth century. On 30 May 1913, the *Doncaster Chronicle* reported that suffragists had attempted to blow up the untenanted Wheatley Hall. A window on the Hall's ground floor was forced and the latch unfastened. Also, a heavy iron bar which held the shutters, was wrenched off. Inside the Hall, a quantity of suffragist literature, soaked in paraffin, was found. But for the failure of the fuse attached to a makeshift bomb, placed beneath the oak staircase, an explosion would have followed.

Around 1914, the Hall, together with the estate, was leased by Sir William Cooke, to the Wheatley Golf Club. Certain sections of the Hall were converted into flats, and the remainder used by the golf club as its club house. The club moved to Armthorpe during the early 1930s, the Hall being demolished around 1933.

Situated south of Wadworth, Wilsic Hall dates from the eighteenth century, probably from the period 1720-1740. It is likely that it occupies the site of a smaller house, one of Tudor origin. The owners of the House have included the Tofield family, the Barnsley Co-operative Society and, during the Second World War, Lt. Griffith. In later years it was a county club but is now occupied by a school.

THE WOODLANDS. S.E

ADWICK.LE.STREET

Miller (1804) notes that Woodlands, in the parish of Adwick, was built by Thomas Bradford, who sold it, with a small quantity of adjoining land, to Christopher Waterton. In a *Doncaster Gazette* sale notice of 14 May 1819, the House is described as a substantial elegant mansion, presenting a handsome and uniform elevation, replete with small stabling for eight horses, coach and gig houses, courtyard, farmyard, barn, granary, cart horse, stable, cow houses, cattle sheds, piggery, poultry houses and numerous other requisite out-offices. Regarding the House's name, Gordon Smith in the *Doncaster Gazette*, 13 January 1966, records that this small mansion was sometimes known as Woodlands Hall, though it is properly called the Woodlands. He also says: 'Although the architecture of this house, is not in the highest classical taste, it is well proportioned, being built of red brick (now covered white) the centre block being headed by a three bay pediment. The ground floor possesses two large stone bay windows, which appear to have been a larger addition.' Thomas Walker was one of the House's noted occupants. He died aged eighty-two in 1891 and his obituary in the *Doncaster Gazette*, 1 April of the same year, notes that he was one of the oldest magistrates of the West Riding, having been appointed in 1854. 'When the Parish church at Adwick was restored some years ago Mr Walker took a deep interest in the work and liberally subscribed to the cost. The model farm buildings in the village were erected by him, which add so much to the neat and trim appearance of the place. He was always ready to promote the welfare of those around him and those he employed on his estate have lost a kind master, and the poor in Adwick, a good friend.' During the twentieth century, the Woodlands has become the Park Club.

Situated between Edenthorpe and Dunsville, Wyndthorpe Hall or Park Lane Hall was built around the early nineteenth century. For a number of years the Wright family resided there and it was later acquired by the Chetwynds, changing the House's name from Park Lane Hall to Wyndthorpe Hall. The *Doncaster Chronicle*, 21 March 1919, revealed: 'Lord and Lady Chetwynd have resided at Wyndthorpe for a large number of years. His lordship took the mansion in 1901; was married in 1904 and purchased the premises in 1906. The residence was known as Park Lane Hall, but was re-christened by its owner. Wynd is the Scotch word for lane, and is also the second syllable of the family name. So in calling the Hall, Wyndthorpe, Viscount Chetwynd preserved a portion of its old title and introduced part of his own name as well.'

In 1919, the Chetwynds sold the Hall along with the estate to the Mutual Cooperative Society for around £20,000, to establish a dairy farm.

By 1949, the Hall was in the hands of West Riding Council and used as a children's home. The *Doncaster Gazette*, 31 May 1951, noted: 'Where once gay and colourful crowds paraded at fashionable garden parties and admired the lawns and flower beds of Wyndthorpe Hall, little children now romp and play in happy contentment. Some are without parents, some have parents who have lost interest in their welfare, and at least two have a mother who is ill in hospital. But one thing each child has in common—a good home where the daily routine is wisely planned and followed with care.' The Hall presently houses a nursing home. The two pictures show Lord and Lady Chetwynd, in full robes, at a function preumably held in the Hall grounds.